True Stories of Autistic and Handicapped Students

"In the Begining was Tommy Allen"

Paul E. Joos

authorHOUSE®

AuthorHouse™
1663 Liberty Drive, Suite 200
Bloomington, IN 47403
www.authorhouse.com
Phone: 1-800-839-8640

First published by AuthorHouse 12/1/2008

ISBN: 978-1-4389-3479-2 (sc)

Printed in the United States of America
Bloomington, Indiana

This book is printed on acid-free paper.

Dedication

To Megan Peca, the cutest Southern
Bell, East or West of the Mississippi. The
Inspiration for me and for anybody who
meets her. Smart as a whip, she can take
it and she can dish it out. A young lady
who never lets the sour side of life get her
down. We should all try to be more like
her.

Chapter 1
Tommy

Tommy Allen was a boy about 10 years old. I never found out exactly how old he was. I only knew him for a few days, but he made a lasting impression on me. He was my first exposure to the world of the mentally handicapped.

I had nothing to do at school between classes, and a friend of mine at the college had asked me several times if I wouldn't mind coming over to the facility (mental institution) which was just next door from the school. I had always hesitated as I had heard of some of the worst stories about the people that were patients there. I was more afraid then anything.

I had decided that the next time that my friend asked that I would go with her and find out for myself what the truth was about what I have heard. At the time I was an Agriculture student, and not a very good one at that. There was always time between classes of which I usually wasted sleeping in the quad or feeding the Koi fish by the dorms.

A few weeks had gone by and I had hunted down my friend instead of her finding me. I wanted to go visit the facility and maybe help if I could.

I met Debbie at the main gate. You needed a pass to get on the grounds or have someone walk you on. I didn't know that this would be the day that would change my life, forever.

We walked by the security office and by the wards where the patients or what they were commonly called "clients" slept and stayed.. We went to her classroom. Room number three. The classrooms were schools for the handicapped run by the county, the district and the facility.

As we walked by the rooms before we got to hers, I noticed a boy, a smaller boy but obviously about ten or eleven years old. He was sitting outside his room leaning against his class door. He was very quiet and seemed to be off into another world. I said hi to him but he made no noise or gesture. I would find out soon that it was often that he was like that. Debbie and I went into her room where her students were already sitting. Her teachers aide was taking care of the class till she got back with me. We weren't inside for three minutes when I started hearing a stinging banging. It was a hollow continuous whamming. It was a persistent and well timed pow!. It never missed a beat, never off a millisecond. Debbie never made one mention of the noise, the banging . By now the thunderous beat had been going on for over an hour. It didn't seem to bother the other students. They never looked up once from the art project they were busy on.

I was hesitant to ask any questions about anything as not to appear ignorant, but I really was, ignorant that is.

In a split second the banging I had been hearing for the past hour or so, stopped. The door of the classroom opened slowly and Tommy Allen walked in and sat down and started doing the activity we were working on, making a paste and draw thing. Tommy talked to us just as though he never had been banging his head. He was just like any other kid you would meet in the neighborhood. Tommy finished his project with the other students. The shuttle was there to pick them up to go back to the hospital wards where he lived and shared his life with other students.

Tommy's' head banging was not his only vice. Tommy would more often than not have a piece of string or rubber band in his hand and would wrap them around his finger or wrist. He would do this over and over. He was a slick little thief. He would always find something to wrap around his finger. He would often take a piece of loose thread from his clothing if he couldn't find anything else. His favorite wrapping was the a rubber band. Over and over, back and forth loosen and tighten.

Tommy had gotten a hold of a rubber band the night after I had first met him. He had snuck a rubber band into the wards and evidently hid it in his under wear. That night he had been wrapping it around his pinky. He had gotten it extra tight . He fell asleep with it around his finger and when he woke up his finger was nearly gone. He had had the rubber band on too long and the doctor had to remove his finger. I saw Tommy one more time after that and he was banging his head very hard. "They" decided to keep him in the ward for the duration which was probably the rest of his life. I would never forget Tommy. He was a unique individual. He was locked in his irrational self.

I would still hear his head banging in my sleep for years. I never found out what happened to Tommy, though I did find out much later that Tommy had a condition with his skull. His skull was so thick and he had so many concusions over his short years that he was unable to harm himself much, at least in his head. Tommy Allen was autistic.

Chapter 2
Boy On The Swing

Tommy was the first special kid I would meet but he would certainly not be the last. The institution I was volunteering at had a rather large park. It was called "Rustic Camp". After a few months of being there helping and sometimes just being in the way, our class went to rustic camp.

The noises Tommy banging his head against the steel door was not the only sound one would hear. It was certainly the loudest but the background was always filled with odd unrecognizable sounds. Before going to rustic camp which was part of the facility, on stepping outside the classroom I heard a noise I thought I recognized but it wasn't clear. I heard the sound before. It was a squeak, long and sustained ,stopped, started again but a slightly different squeak or a creek. Each repeated itself over and over. The class was walking slowly to camp some distance away. I could see a person on a large swing. There were six swings on one large "A" frame. They were all empty but one swing was occupied. Our whole class was together. Many of them I do not remember. We approached closer to the person on the swing. His back was to us. He was swinging very high, almost to the point of being dangerous. The squeaking was coming from the swing. Back and forth squeak, creek, squeak. It only then that we, myself ,Debbie and the rest of the class noticed the obvious, the boy who was more of a young adult was absolutely naked and not a stitch of clothing was on him. There was a pile of clothing next to the swing. He was going back and forth, very high and he was holding the swing chain with one hand. We had past him by this time and as the others I was paying no attention. It seemed that the boy on the swing was a daily scene, commonplace. I turned my back to look at him as we were a bit closer to the camp. He was swinging and holding on the chain with one hand. With the other hand he was…. well…what he was doing, he was doing it with the rhythm of the swing. The visual memory of the boy on the swing is firm in my mind but the sound is yet another. To this day every time I hear a swing at a park or school, the first thing that pops in my mind is the young man in the swing. I saw him nearly every time I went to help. Everyday

I could hear the swing in the background. For the next year or so on my visit's the boy on the swing was there nearly everyday. He never disappointed us. Fact is I never saw him out of the swing.

Chapter 3
Kami

I have been giving my time for about three months. We had made several trips to Rustic camp. It never failed that something would happen on the way to camp or when we were there.

Debbies class had prepared a picnic which was actually their lunch that was delivered to class each day. We took there lunches and packed them in one big basket to look like a picnic.

On our way, our boy on the swing did not disappoint us. He was there swinging away. We walked through the camp gates and found a few benches to sit at. The students were let to roam the park. There was no where to escape, it was a very secure place and there was one way in and one way out. There were peacocks, chickens, a couple of cats, and an old, old pig. The pig was huge but harmless. The park also housed two large donkeys. They were old and only had half their teeth. The donkeys were very tame and the kids could do almost anything to them.

The kids picnic was a peanut butter sandwich, an apple, a couple of cookies, milk and maybe a fruit cup. All the students ate everything. They especially scarfed up the cookies. We always had extra cookies.

Kami was a little smaller than average girl. She was very pale with dark hair. Kami could not talk any more than a few mumbled and unintelligible words. She would always smile as she would make her slow but shuffling walk through and around the park. On this day Kami ate her lunch at the table. She had some chips, her sandwich, and a handful of cookies. She was about finished and she got up, she reached across the table and took an apple. When she got up she shuffled away from us about 30 feet or so and stood there with her apple. We did not pay that much attention to her other than one of the donkeys was slowly walking toward her. The donkeys loved to be petted, they seemed to know the students better than I did. They knew exactly which ones would stand and scratch and pet them. We had our eyes off of her and the rest of the students. They were all off running around or sitting enjoying the nice day.

Debbie and I were off in our own conversation. Debbies assistant was reading a magazine. I think the park trip was more for us than it was for the students.

Ten minutes or so passed and it seemed that we might as well look up and see what the kids were doing. The donkey had come over to Kami and was licking her apple. Kami had allowed the half toothless donkey to take a bite from the apple. We went back to doing what we were doing which was enjoying the day at the camp talking and having a few cookies for ourselves.

I had some intuition to look over at Kami to see what she was up to. I saw Kami and I saw the donkey, but didn't see the right side of Kami. I couldn't see where her right arm was. Kami was very close if not right up to the animal. I was a little concerned although Debbie sat there not worried.

I got up and the minute I had a better look I realized where Kamis' arm was. The donkey had taken the apple from Kami. The problem was that the apple was still attached to Kamis' hand. Her arm was all the way to her shoulder inside and buried in the mouth of the donkey. At first I thought this is not a good thing. I went to where they were standing and held Kamis' arm as much as I could because the rest of it was shoulder to lips of the donkey. I pulled slowly and her arm came out, sliding. At the end of her hand was the apple still held onto. Her arm was slippery, coated with the slime of donkey saliva.

The apple still had just the first initial nibble. We took the apple from Kami and gave it to the donkey without the arm attached. Kami took awhile to clean off but she was happy enough to sit at the table and eat some more cookies.

Kami was only thirteen and later after I had long stopped going to the hospital to help, I found that she had died from her degenerative condition. She had tubular sclerosis as best I can remember. Although there is still more to tell about my friends at the hospital, and I will. I kept in contact for a couple of years with Debbie and others that worked there.

Chapter 4
Mitchel

Mitchel has a long history in my involvment with special kids. He was mostly quiet and almost invisible in the class. He would sit and rock at his seat and make little whinning noises off and on. He was 10 years old. He was a tall and extra thin. I knew how old he was as well as the other students because we had a birthday board next to the calendar. He was very messy. During art projects, especially painting he was a living disaster, but he seemed happy. He rarely got out of his seat. We had to prompt him up "come on Mitchel lets go". I paid little attention to him.

Lunch time came and the meals were being delivered to the class on hospital type trays. Each student got their lunch as they sat waiting. Mitchel always sat in the back row of the class and when he ate he was very quiet. There were four rows of tables and four or five students per row.

I was kneeling on one knee behind a student, helping with lunch. Out of nowhere a student from one of the back rows stood up quickly and quietly stepped behind me, bit me with great force on the meaty part of the top of the shoulder. He latched on and didn't let go. I fell to the ground a couple of seconds later and the skin on my shoulders snapped from his mouth.

When I looked up, (I was flat on my back) Mitchel was starring straight down at me. He was looking at me as though nothing had happened. He reached over and took the extra bag of chips from the students lunch I was helping. It seems Mitchel didn't get his bag of chips. Debbie was out of the room using the restroom and when she came back she saw the desks disshovled. Me, I was grabbing my shoulder and it hurt. Mitchel went back and sat down quietly. Debbies only comment was "what the hell happened"? Was sorry to tell her I hadn't a clue, but that Mitchel felt it necessary to bite me for a bag of chips.

Debbie forgot to tell me that Mitchel had to have lunch first. By not giving his first was only compounded by the fact the other student had two bags of chips. Mitchel was always calculating, always observing never missing a thing. Even when he was rocking back an forth making his little noises and starring off into la la land he was recording everything. Mitchels' day was structured in his own mind. The day had to have order, nothing misplaced, nothing out of sequence.

I looked up in the files what was wrong with Mitchel and all his diagnosis would reveal was that he had a dysfunctional disorder. That ment that they really didn't know why he was the way he was. As time went by Mitchel and I would have intermittent confrontations. I would win some, Mitchel would win some. It was always over food. Mitchel would surface again many years down the road.

Chapter 5
Short But Moving

Things at the institution were always busy. Each of the half dozen or so class rooms around us were always going somewhere or doing something. I thought it was odd that nearly every patient over 16 years old was a smoker. Cigarettes to them was gold and were only allowed a certain amount each day. They were used as bribes and rewards to get them to comply. Remember this is early 70's. Our students never got cigarettes, they were still much too young.

It was difficult to keep an eye on your own students and other patients. At times one or more might wonder off and there would be an alert put out. Security would scramble about looking everywhere until everyone was accounted for. One student came up missing in the afternoon roll call. All of ours were accounted for. Security was going from room to room and ward to ward to find a small but as they put it very strong

boy. Earlier, the teacher in another class, the one that was missing the student reported that she had her teachers desk missing. Their class had been off to the park.
Her desk was large, all wood but it had caster wheels so the custodians could move it for vacuuming.

The boy and desk were missing for over an hour. Somehow they were related. The security department was starting to scramble more. A missing student is not good.

The missing boy was finally sighted nearly an hour and a half after the report. At the same moment the missing desk was found. The boy had been forgotten in the class room as the others went to the park. For whatever reason he had, he decided he would move the teachers desk from the classroom to wherever he was going. He had pushed the desk from the classroom nearly a half mile.

He was headed toward the main gate, through a network of back alleys. The wheels were making a screeching noise and wobbling clatter. No one paid any attention, he looked like he knew what he was doing. I can only visualize this small boy pushing a teachers desk five times his size down an alley over a half mile across the busy facility.

The teacher of course never heard the

end of it. She did get into some trouble but those kind of things happened all the time. The first thing the teacher looks for now is that her desk is in the classroom.

Chapter 6
Gone From The Institution:
Martha Smith

Martha Smith was the principal of the school at Pacific State Hospital as it was called when I volunteered. Martha was the principal of all of the special ed sites in a huge area. She ruled the schools with an iron fist but she was always fair. Martha was in here late 60s. Still working and full of vinegar. She always wore a large straw hat to protect her face from the sun and carried with her a large straw bag. She carried it all of her school with stuff in the bag, and it was always packed to the hilt. She reminded me of a homeless old woman. Martha had visited the school at Pacific State many times when I was there. She never said much to me. There were other volunteers and I was just another face in the crowd. I had been volunteering off and on for about a year. Martha made one of her unannounced visits. She would go from class to class. There were six classrooms. She would stop and talk to each teacher for awhile, look around and see if everything was going okay. She came into Debbies room where we were doing another art project. We did a lot of art projects. Martha saw me, turned and asked Debbie some questions that I couldn't hear but I knew they were about me. Martha came to me and asked if I would step outside, she wanted to talk to me.. She wanted to know who I was and basically what I was doing there. Then she asked me the big question.She asked me if I wanted a job, and actually get paid for working with these great bunch of kids. I found out later that Martha did know who I was and what I was doing there, Debbie had told her.

Remember I was going to school to be an agriculture teacher. I loved those students that I worked with but wasn't sure if I wanted to make a career of them. Then again I could sure use the money. I decided that I would jump through the hoops and try to get the job Martha was recommending me for. It wasn't long after I took the test and interviews that I was hired. I was assigned a position at San Jose School in West Covina. It was a school with five hundred give or take a few, Mentally handicapped students, many of them

Autistic. I never could have imagined that there were so many, much less so many in one place. Marthas office was at San Jose School and from then on I saw here often. There was more to my being hired than just being a good worker. Turns out that that there were very few men working in the schools with the mentally handicapped. Of the three hundred that applied for the few openings there were only three men. I was hired and Martha always kept me in check.

Chapter 7
Teachers Aide and Steve S

I was hired to be a teachers aide. I worked with a man who was quite heavy, firm but well liked by everyone. He knew how to handle the hard to handle kids and we had fun at doing our job. I still had problems that we actually got paid for doing what we did. We taught the students their ABC's how to add or even how to count. Most of them would forget what they did or learned the next day so there was a lot of repetitive activities.

Every week Mike (the teacher) and I would dump a large container of nuts and bolts on the huge table we had in the middle of the classroom. The students would sort and separate all day till the hundreds of nuts and bolts were two piles of nuts and bolts. When the students finished they got a party. For two years this was the routine. Every once in a while our class would walk to the donut shop and on big occasions we would walk to the Deli and the students would buy sandwiches and sodas. In those two years little happened other than that. I learned who these special people were and I was becoming more and more aware that this is where my lifes direction was going.

Steven S was a student of ours. For the likes of me I couldn't figure out why he was at our school. We had mentally high kids and the very lowest, but Steven didn't seem to fit into any category. Steven had a drivers license and drove a small motorcycle to school. He couldn't read but I checked it out and he had a valid license. We didn't have a policy of mentally handicapped students not to drive so we just accepted it. As with many students they had friends and relationships with other students that went to our school. Many of them lived close to each other. Steven knew some of the girls on our campus. The girls he knew best were from one family. As we found out later he frequented the house of these girls often. There were nine girls from this one family and every one of them was going through our school or had been at one time or another. Steven came to school one day with a handful of pictures. He was showing some other students his pictures and they were all laughing. I was very curious, and asked Steven if I could see the pictures. He tried to hide them by putting them in his pocket but I insisted. He grudgingly took them out and handed to me. His face immediately showed red with embarrassment. I looked and was surprised to see naked pictures of Steven and two of the girls and they were quite involved, if you know what I mean. I shared the pictures with the teacher I was working with. He shared them with the principal who shared them with both sets of parents who shared them with the police. By all indications nothing happened to Steve or the girls, but Steven did not go to there house anymore. Steven stayed at our school for one more year riding his small motorcycle. He fell out of site when he was transferred to a regular high school program for the mentally handicapped. I did see him occasionally on his bike zipping down the street going to school as I was going to work.

I was doing well in school and still taking classes like tractors and fertilizers. I had one class: Organic Chemistry that I had taken two other times and flunked miserably. I know this is not my story but its how I got from point A to point B. It did not look as though I was going to pass Organic Chemistry so I needed to make a life decision. I wanted to teach, but I needed the degree. I decided to take Psychology/ Sociology. I had all the units I needed for electives and it was only a year and a half later that I took extra unit's and full time Saturday classes.

Martha was following my progress all along and had different plans for me. Maybe she saw something in me that I didn't. Her plan was to get me graduated and hire me as a "Permit Teacher", which is a teacher but not fully credentialed. Her eventual plan was to get me fully credentialed as a "Severelly Handicapped " teacher.

I had Graduated with a B.S. in Behavioral Science. Martha had immediately offered me a position as a a teacher in the development center. Seeing I wasn't going anywhere with the Agriculture degree and I really did love those special kids, I took the job.

Chapter 8
Dianna

It is not my intention to gross people out or sensationalize my experience with these special students, its just what happened.

The development center was a separate building from the rest of the school. There were eight open classrooms. Each teacher had at least a small view what the other teacher was doing. My frist day in the development center was a baptism of fire. I was now the teacher. The environment was one of a soap opera. There was lots of gossip and chit chat. I had not met my students and as for the past two years I had not ever been inside the development center. I arrived at work extra early the first day to meet my students. I looked at their names on the role sheet and I had only seven students. How hard could that be?

Each student arrived on a special bus. When they arrived I had to ask the bus driver who they were. I slowly sorted them all out with the help of the other teachers. All seven were there. I had four in wheel chairs and three walkers. Dianna was the last one off of the bus. The schedule was very simple. Bring them to the bathroom, give them a morning snack, bathroom, lunch, bathroom, afternoon snack, bathroom. Much of their day was back and forth from the bathroom. In between bathroom we had art activities and mobility activities. For the most part my students were very low mentally functioning. Every student needed most everything done for them including taking care of their diaper. Most of them wore diapers. There was lots of diaper changing.

Dianna was the last one off of the bus and she was my first student. Most of the time my aide who was a female changed and took care of the girls and I took care of the boys. This time Mary my aide wasn't there. She was at the school office and I needed to take Dianna to the bathroom. I had watched Mary take her earlier and did what she did. Pants down, diaper off, sit down.The doors to the bathroom were always open so at least you could see the feet of the person in the bathroom. You could not see there hands.

I left Dianna alone for a few minutes with her feet still visible from the classroom. Dianna was very quiet. She appeared to be doing her business and was leaving her there for a few more minutes. Mary was still not back yet.

Dianna was a big girl for her age, she was thirteen years old with the mentality of a one year old. She would rock back and forth from morning till she got back on the bus. She would rock while she was on the toilet, though she was very very quiet. She was quiet that is until she was done using the bathroom and then she would let out a scream. She let out her chilling scream. It took me about two minutes to get to her so I could drop what I was doing with the other students. By the time I got into the bathroom Dianna had done the unthinkable. She had used the restroom, but she didn't leave things alone. She had taken the product (Poop!) from the toilet and smeared it all over herself. She had poop all over herself and the wall. She had it in her mouth and her hair, everywhere but where I could see her from outside the bathroom. If this wasnt bad enough. She had of course started her period, so to add to the finger painting was her mentruation, also in her hair and on the wall and everywhere. I didn't quite know what to do. I had students getting up and walking around the classroom and getting into things. Wheel chair students suddenly came alive and were pushing their chairs into the wall. I couldn't leave Dianna or she would make a bigger mess than she already had.

Mary finally made it back from the office where she was turning in the daily paper work. Mary just chuckled when she saw the disaster. She told me that she would watch the the students in the classroom and get them straightened out while I cleaned up Dianna and the bathroom. Some how it didn't seem fair but I guess I deserved it. It took me almost an hour to erase all the evidence from the bathroom and Dianna. It was a baptism of fire. If I could do that, I could do anything. It was Marys way of indoctrinating me to this special world. She would never allow me to have to do that again, at least alone. Mary had her way of things She was a Mexican angel. For two years she brought me up right. She taught me patients, tolerance and a humbling perspective of the children that we were given the responsibility for.

Chapter 9
Wally

"Each person in our world is an individual but we are still more alike than we are different" This was something a professor at my college said when I was finishing my credentials as a special ed teacher. It didn't make much sense then but it does now. Some of the best friends I ever made were those of the mentally handicapped. Although I have witnessed the bizarre and down right weird I still see that there is that similarity in them which we all process. I realized that after the years I was volunteering at the mental institution and my shaky beginning at San Jose School. I learned very quickly that everyone needs to depend on each other. It is a team effort. Every teacher has something unique to contribute to the rest, and there is always another teacher somewhere that is better than you are. All of this seemed to come to me as a virtual significant moment, a self actualizing state of mind.

The first few days of my babtism of fire with Dianne showed me the obvious, they needed me and I needed them. These cherabums were becoming the center of the universe for me. They were the pull of gravity, they were only second to my own children.

Tommy was only the first and Dianne was certainly significant, but there were many friends yet to meet. There were to be hundreds of students that were to be at least for a minute, an hour, or year that would be part of the experience.

Wally was one of those students. He didn't make the big impression, he wasn't particularly close to me or me him. It was something he did. For some reason I just never forgot it. Our class, the same one Dianne was in had many outside activities including swinging, relaxing, playing with the yard ball, and bar-b-queing. When all else failes, Bar-B-Que!

The students all loved the out door eating. To them it seemd like something special. It was the anticipation of something a little bit different. Mary was preparing the garnishes and side dishes for the students. The students were not quite able to do much of that for themselves.. So I got the fire going and got the outdoor table ready. Mary did the rest. Everyone would patiently wait. Some of them were outside under the tree while some were inside napping. The menu was hotdogs and chips with all the trimmings. The school supplied the food and got the hot dogs in bulk. They came in a five pound box. Mary had opened the box and left them on the shelf by the door of the class room so I could get to them easily when the fire was ready. Mary and I were going back and forth inside and outside of the class. Mary stopped and talked with me for awhile outside for a couple of minutes.. three minutes or less. When I went back in to get the hot dogs Wally had walked over edging his way ever so slowly, waiting for the chance to pounce on the five pound box. Within minutes Wally had downed over half of the box.. He was pushing hotdogs into his mouth and down his throat so fast he barely took a chew. Mind you these were not the small little things. These were the big baseball park style. Wally was shaking and pushing those things in as fast as he possibly could. I grabbed the box, I got Mary and told her what Wally was doing, or did. I thought Wally would have gotten sick but all he did was follow me outside and was wanting more. Wally did not get one more hotdog. We kept our eye on him the rest of the day but he showed no ill effect. There was enough food for the rest of the kids and we finished our day. Wally would always be on our watch list and even though he would try to swipe food off and on he never got away with it again. Wally had a functional disorder, some kind of brain damage. And who knows maybe hotdog overdose.

Chapter 10
Rickey

No doubt about it Rickey was my favorite student. Teachers hate to admit it, especially teachers of the handicapped but we all have our favorites. Rikey was my favorite by a long shot. They each had there own special place in my heart but Rickey latched onto mine and wouldn't let go. Odd thing about Rickey he never did anything so outrageously bizarre or crude. He was just an innocent bystander in his infliction which so many kids had in the seventies. He was a Down Syndrome boy. His favorite past time was sitting Indian style on the classroom floor holding his two fore fingers on each hand in front of his eyes and waving them as fast as he could. He would make grunting and groaning noises, laugh and give a big raspberry to the air. Self indulged and self stimulated as he was he never let me out of his sight.

Some images never leave your mind.

Rickey went to the County fair with the rest of the students one year. I think it was 1981. L.A. County Fair, in Pomona. We had all ten students.

It wasn't easy keeping them all together. Mary and I had a couple of college student helpers of our own and they paired off with the students so they never got out of our sight.I always wondered if those college students did what I did and fell in love with those kids or got scared off. Rikey saw a small horse at the petting zoo that was tied up for pony rides. He really perked up and wouldn't leave the pony alone. He saw some other kids ride the pony, one after the other. I didn't think I would get him out of there until he got to ride. Rickey never showed any real emotion unless he was doing his little finger thing. He never showed a lot of outward emotion. He didntnt like holding hands or touching. Although he followed me around like a little puppy dog he didn't like contact. Rickey grabbed my hand and brought it toward the pony. It took Rickey a lot of fortitude to do that. I decided I would let him ride the pony. I put my two bucks in. I threw him up on the horse and the lady who was in charge led him around in a small circle. Rikey was laughing and smiling, he even put his fingers in front of his face and waved them like I never have seen him before. That is the image I will never forget.

Twenty years later I was going through some old photos and Rickey jumped up out of the pile of pictures. It was like it was just happening. It was Rickey riding the pony. He was sitting straight up and looking proud, smiling, grunting his Rickey noise,. I could hear it in my memory. Regardless of the picture I just found, I had that image in my mind for as many years and it would never leave me. I would never forget the image or the sounds I heard that day. It was the sound of happiness.

Chapter 11
Marky

Although Rickey liked to follow me around, he had a friend named Marky who was also a small down syndrome litlle boy. Rickey had black hair dark brown eyes and freckles. Marky on the other hand had blonde hair, blue eyes and the most fairest of skin. They were the opposite mirror image of each other. They might of well be called frick and frack. Sometimes they would have a spat and fight over a silly little toy, but mostly they were very close. Marky would usually never come over to me with Rickey. He was much more the loner with the exception of Rickey. They lived in the same foster home and would ride on the same bus, eat with each other at the lunch table, and play with the same toys with each other. As small as they were they both had voracious appetites. They ate breakfast, snack, lunch, snack, and probably had breakfast before they even got to school.

Marky and Rickey, what a pair! the two of them reminded me of a pair salt and pepper shakers.

One day Marky came to school but didn't seem to be himself. He kind of stayed by himself and didn't play with Rickey with the same enthusiasm as usual. They had their usual snack and later lunch. Of course they both had their daily five times in the bathroom, and I think in some respects that was their favorite time of day. After lunch Marky laid down and took a nap. He didn't do that very often. Sometimes all of the students would get very tired of a hard day of playing and lay down on a mat and sleep for hours. It was the end of the day and Mary and I got the kids up and ready for the bus. Rikey was raring to go but Marky was still lagging a bit. I thought maybe he had a touch of the flue. It was hard for them because they arent like normal kids that can tell you their tummy hurts or they have a sore throat. Marky got on the bus and sat down. I could see his little face in the window of the bus. He didn't have his normal smirk or devilish smile, he just had his head down. He gave one little look up. Rikey was sitting next to him on the inside isle of the bus but I could see his head bobbing up and down and the silhouette of his fingers waving wildly in front of his eyes. The bus took off.

Mary and I were busy picking up and cleaning the toys as was our duty after the students left. They would slobber and put things in their mouths. The diaper pail was always full and we had to give the room a thourough disinfection everyday. It took a good half an hour to go through the room, we were almost done and the teacher next door came in our room to tell me I had a phone call. I went to the office we all shared and picked up the phone. Marks' foster Mom had called and asked what I had given Marky to eat during the day. It seems he had been coughing up and choking when he got home. I told her nothing different and also that he didn't seem to be feeling well or not acting like the Marky that we usually know. She seemed satisfied but was concerned at the same time.

I usually stayed after school to finish the clean up and get caught up with the tons of paper work. Mary had left to go home. I was just finishing up and the phone rang in the office. I went to pick it up hoping it wasn't going to be one of those long drawn out parent calls that I didn't mind but sometimes at the end of the day you just want to get home. It was Markys' foster Mom. She seemed to be sad and she stalled at her speech. She began to tell me that Marky had just past away. He had a heart attack. It was totally unexpected. He never had any history of heart problems. He just past away that quick. Markys little face in the window of the bus would be the last time I would see him. I never took pictures of Marky like I did Rikey. I dug around and did not find one. I only had my memory of him.

Chapter 12
Kenny

I was beginning to learn that death and dealing with it was part of the job. The students in many ways were fragile and in many ways not in the greatest health. One could never be sure that there wasn't another Marky waiting to happen. Debbie by this time had been assigned to my school. She told me that she had lost several students over the years but didn't talk about it much. She told me not to get too close to the students or you can have your heart broken. I think by that time it was already too late. All of the students were like my own. These weren't regular students and we weren't regular teachers. We were their Mommy, Daddy, Nurse, Doctor, Teacher, Chef and Advocate all rolled up into one. Kenny was another student that sort of just fit into the crowd. He didn't make much noise or get in the way. He would stand there and make silly gestures with his hands. He didn't move unless he was coaxed and if you pushed him to go to fast he would sit down. Kenny was part of the classroom fixture. He fed himself and rarely made a potty accident. He enjoyed our company but didn't go out of his way to be with us when the rest of the class was doing an art project or playing with table toys. Kennys Mom was a very nice person. She was always interested in the things we were doing but wasn't overbearing or have unrealistic ideas that Kenny was going to all of a sudden become normal. Kenny was in my class for about a year, he was there everyday. I could always depend on Kenny to be there. Friday, Mary and I always did a little extra clean up and go for the weekend. Kenny got on the bus and went home with the other students. He was happy.

Monday morning comes early it seems and Mary was there before I was. Mary had bad news. Kenny had died late Sunday with heart attack. He died just one month from when Marky succumbed to the same thing. I didn't know at that time if this was what I wanted to go through for the rest of my working life. Mary assured me like she always does that these children needed us and that we were the best people for the job. I was beginning to think though that I was the one that needed them more. Two days later two children from a class room next to us that I did not know very well were killed in a freeway accident. I only asked myself, when does it end? As Markys and Kennys picture was found among many nearly twenty five years later. We never heard from Kennys Mom again. She lived alone with him and took care of him until he died.

Chapter 13
Missi

Missis' picture wasn't hard to find. She had a tongue on her that she could turn upside down, touch her chin, and then touch the top of her nose. The picture I have of her she is doing just that. Her favorite past time. She had the habit of of persistently repeating her name, grab her own tongue, twist it around and repeat her name ten or twenty times. At the time Missi was 15 years old. When she walked it was always dragging her toes. She wore her shoes out quite often. Missi had large busts which she was grabbing as often as her tongue. Even at that Missi was a good kid to have around. She was always friendly. She was tagging along and shadowing Mary and me constantly. When Mikey wasn't there Missi was. Missi had one bad habit or I should say a remarkable ability. She could spit. Not just spit but she could role up her tongue and fling one small ball of spit with pin point accuracy and she could do it over and over. Especially when she was up set she could rattle off thirty spit's a minute. Missi was usually well behaved but she had her moments. If she did not want to move or go with the group she would sit and spit. Walking with in her range was a real hazard.

Many times I would go home spat upon and nearly drenched. I would take a shower the minute I got home but more often than not I had college class right after work. I must have been disgusting.

Missi was afraid of nothing although she was stubborn she had no fear, but one thing. Missi feared plastic animals. I didn't know this until one day our school got in an order of toys that the administrator ordered. One of the boxes was a bunch of large plastic farm animals. Our class was the recipient of the "farm". Mary and I opened the boxes in front of the students. They liked surprises. The first box we opened was a huge cow. When we opened it, it was still wrapped in paper. Missi was sitting at the table where we opened them. I let Missi tear off the paper from the cow. I knew it was a cow because it said cow on the wrapping. Missi took off the paper stared and screamed at the top of her lungs. She started crying got up from the table and you guessed it, started spitting. She wrang her hands behind her back and backed off to a comfortable distance. Missi was never the same. She always kept an eye open for the cabinete that the animals were kept in, and we never took them out unless she was absent or out of the room. Her mother was also surprised as Missi had many stuffed animals at home and played with them regularly. The animals in our classroom were very life like. I think that she was afraid of them because she was very confused. Although she saw the other students play with them she never got over her fear. Missi would use the bathroom like all the other students, It was a bathroom prolifery. She would always sit on the thrown with her legs crossed and liked (pretend) reading or at least looking at her favorite magazine. If you let her she could spend the whole day sitting on the can and looking at pictures. My last glimpse of Missi was her, looking out of the bus window with her tongue wrapped around her nose. Maybe not the prettiest picture but one that was lasting.

Chapter 14
Steven C

Each day for our snack the whole class would sit at a giant table that we used for arts and crafts, school stuff and just to gather to get our thoughts together when things seemed to be falling apart. Mary and I could sit there while the kids were on the toilet and the rest were napping. The bathroom and the rest of the classroom were all visible and we could monitor each student.

Steven loved snack time and he particularly liked sitting at the table. He spent most of his day there or in the bathroom. He was one of the strangest students that I ever taught. Steven was very skinny and appeared incredibly fragile. He had never uttered a word or made any kind of verbal noise, grunt or groan. He never communicated in any way. He never gestured, pointed or touched to make a tap on the shoulder. Steven would just sit like a monument until the crackers and juice showed up. He would help himself, put his cookie on a napkin and daintily hold his cup, But he wasn't drinking juice like the rest of the kids. He drank coffee, Mary and I would have a cup of coffee while the class had there break. Steven had coffee with us. He would prepare his own cup. Carefully he would put two teaspoons of sugar and a dash of cream. He would sip his coffee politely and ever so neatly. Steven had the best of etiquette but when the coffee was gone Steven was gone too, more mentally gone then physically. Steven had something much older about him. He had a stooped over walk and walked with his palms of his hands facing backward. He had a very light covering of dark hair over his entire body. His eyebrows were very heavy and black. The one thing that was most noticeable when noticed was that he had a short, for lack of a better description,tail. There were two or three extra vertebrea below his tailbone. Steven had a syndrome called Cornelious Delang and after a little research found that there were only fifty or so individuals that were documented to have his syndrome. Turns out that the main ape in the movie " Planet Of The Apes " was named Cornelious, after the syndrome. Steven seemed very apelike, the hair, the walk, the tail. Steven was like a fixture in our classroom. Most of the time you never knew he was there. Steven was present everyday for school and one day he didn't showup, no explaination, and never showed up again. I missed my coffee partner. Mary was okay but Steven made everyday a little more interesting. And Mary couldn't sit still long enough to have a conversation with anyway.

Chapter 15
Dianne

I had worked in the Development Center for two years Marky, Wally, Missi and a lot of heartbreak. The heartbreak was growing to be part of the job. I finished up getting my degree in psychology, and almost done with my regular teaching credentials. Martha asked me if I wanted to move on to students that were at least a little bit more academically inclined. That September of 1982 started my new class. I had to leave Mary behind. She preferred the Development Center any way and she knew that day would come that I would be moving on. She would need to train another teacher. I had a whole new class although I was a bit familiar with some of the students. Dianne was my first student in this class. A different Dianne but she was unique. She rocked back and forth like Michael in the mental institution. She clicked her teeth together, very lightly but just enough to hear it. For the first three months or so the class was sedate and activities were mostly puzzles, arts and crafts, and group games. Dianne along with her incessant rocking would repeat a word or phrase over and over. When not clicking her teeth she was mumbling "newba" newba, newba, newba. It didn't seem to meen anything and for a month latter she still was repeating the "newba" phrase. Not long from then I noticed Dianne always sat Indian style on her chair, rocking and chatering her teeth and then newba.

I noticed she had very worn shoes. She wore the same shoes everyday. I was surprised when I saw on the bottom of her shoe "newba". Her shoes were worn in a way that the name of the shoe was half worn off and and what should have read New Balance was half scrapped away. Dianne could see the word on the bottom of her shoe sitting the way she did and I could only figure she was reading it . I took her shoes of and let her sit with her socks on. She did not mumble one newba as long as I kept her shoes off. A light went off in my head and I gave her more words one at a time on cards. I would tell her the word and once I told her she never forgot. She could read many of the words without telling her. Dianne amazed me through the year I would work in that class. She learned many words and after time she became more aware of all of us and interacted. She never stopped rocking. Dianne was Autistic. She had an incredible memory but lived in another world most of the time. And she did say newba again as she wore those shoes for the entire year that I worked in that class.

Chapter 16
Sid

November of this same school year our class received a boy named Sid. He had a big head in proportion to his body. He was a good looking boy. He always dressed very well and he always came to school clean. Not all the students came neat and clean. Some didn't shower for days and would come to school in the same clothes day after day. Sid rarely went home clean as our class did a lot of activities that got them dirty. We played hard in the playground and a lot of physical activities in the classroom. We got Sid on a Monday and by his first couple of days I realized that he was not going to talk but he did run off. If your eyes were not peeled on him contiuously he would take off to wherever he could get. He would bolt out of the door and run. The first Thursday morning of Sids week at San Jose School we learned something else. Thursday was the regular day that the crew would come to mow the lawns and take care of the plants. The lawn mower always started at the far end of school. Generally we didn't notice if they were there or not until they went by our classroom. It was a huge tractor with wide blades for mowing a big area at one time. Sid heard the lawn mower coming closer. He covered his ears as though it really bothered him. The tractor and blades were very loud. In a minute the crew was coming by our class. They zoomed by with grass flying in the air, and off in a second to the open field. The mower was off and away where we could barely hear it from the class. Sid could hear it. He got up from his desk in a milisecond got to the door and opened it. Before I could get up to stop him he was long gone half way to the mower. He was chasing it with his arms wildly flailing. I ran to catch him. His intentions were to catch the mower. What he would do if he did catch it? I did not want to know. I ran as hard as I could for what seemed like eons. Sid was laughing outloud and up to that point it was the only verbal noise I heard out of him. I caught up to him and tackled him. He struggled like a student possessed. All he wanted was to get up and chase the lawn mower. With its open blades the mower would have killed him if he reached his destination. The Mower moved on and the guy driving had not a clue what was going on behind him. With the mower out of sight Sid got up calmly and came back to class with me clutching his hand. Every Thursday after that we waited patiently for the lawn crew to come to school. We would block the door with our bodies. Sid would go into a frenzy, kicking, yelling and scratching. I don't know why Sid was so intense over the mower but I did look in his files more deeply what was going on with him, why he was the way he was. When Sid was much younger he got the typical shots kids would get like D.P.T. There is always a chance a person could have a reaction from early childhood vaccinations. Steven was one in about four million that would have as serious a reaction as him. Sids parents had a lawsuit against the company that made the vaccination so they would not comment on it to me but it was for millions of dollars. It would take them already several years from that point till they would get a settlement if any. Steven eventually went on to a special school for the Autistic, hopefully where they did not have lawn mowers.

Chapter 17
Rooster

San Jose School was a school that was always busy. There were well over 500 students all with different degrees of mental disorders or retardation. Our classes were always going on field trips, over night camp outs, walks in the community or parent recitals. One of our functions was to get out into the community, go shopping, ride the city bus and sometimes out to lunch. Many times we would informally combine a couple of classes. Some were higher functioning students some were less capable. I worked at San Jose School for eight years and things never seemed to change. It was the greatest place in the world to work. I loved my job. It seemed unfair to get paid for doing something that you loved doing so much. My class was more lower capable than the one we were going to the Mall with. We were going to go window shopping. It was usually not a fun trip for us as there were many pitfalls and potential problems. We had to keep an extra eye on each student so they wouldn't walk off or get lost. The combined classes were to ride the city bus each student that could, would give their fare for the bus ride. A couple of students were learning how to ride the bus independently and were very capable. These two students had a bus pass to make it a little easier a bit less expensive to ride. Rooster as he was called was to be one of these students and he was to walk to the bus stop with another "capable" student and catch the bus before ours and meet us at the Mall. The walk to the bus stop was just a block away. No problem. The two students left for the bus, Rooster and another. I don't know if I ever knew Roosters real name but his nickname fit him well. He was a small guy and had fire engine red hair and a million red freckles. He had ridden the bus many times by himself and he actually took the city bus home most of the time. He was very careful with his priveledge of being independent. When we got to the bus stop they were gone well on their way to the Mall. They were to wait for us there. The rest of the class boarded the next bus and we started on our way. The bus drivers knew us well as we rode the bus often. They were tolerant of our slow pace getting on the bus. Most of the bus drivers liked the kids and looked forward to having us ride.

The entire class arrived at the Mall. Rooster and his buddy were there waiting patiently. We had all day to shop around. The buses ran on a twenty minute cycle so Rooster and his friend would have to leave that soon before us. After a hard day of looking in windows we had Rooster and friend go to the bus and the rest of us would meet the at the final drop off. The two were on their way and we waited for the next bus. We took our usual twenty minutes to get on and pay but the driver didn't care, he was ahead of schedule. The ride to school was uneventful, that is until we came to the final bus stop. Roosters buddy was standing there but there was no Rooster. We got off the bus and asked where he was. He explained the best he could that he and Rooster got into an argument. Rooster had gotten off at the bus stop before us and said he would catch the next bus. The problem was that there were many routes that traveled to other destinations. Rooster it seems got on a bus to somewhere else. We waited for a half an hour and no Rooster. Both classes went back to school and called the police and the bus company. We put out an APB. Roosters pass was pretty much unlimited in a wide area. By the end of the school day there was still no Rooster.

We drove around town a bit to see if we could spot him. No Rooster. He was not my student. The teacher that went with us to the Mall told me to go ahead a go home, and that he would keep looking and wait at the school. Mike the other teacher called his parents and they went on the search too. I had to go for a class before I got home so I took off. I went to my class and after a long day at work and my college class I was very tired but still concerned about our little redhead. I sat down in front of the T.V. and turned on the news. Just like now I love watching the news. There were a couple of news shorts that came on, I watched them then it happened. A Special Report! Police and parents are searching for a handicapped individual missing in the area of West Covina and the surrounding area. Roosters face appeared on national network T.V. I was bug eyed and could not believe what I was seeing. Mike called me and told me he would call and tell me if they had found him. After the News progranm it wasn't 20 minutes Mike called again and told me they had found him in a donut shop just outside Los Angeles, about 30 miles away. Roosters parents had gone to pick him up. Although His bus explorations were not over, Rooster was to be retrained to ride the bus. Rooster was 18 and sooner or later he would be on his own.

Chapter 18
Winnie and the New School

When Rooster had his excursion it was the end of the school year. I had finished all of my credentials and was on my way. I was a full fledged "Severally Handicapped teacher." I was going to get full teachers pay. In order to fill teachers positions I would need to leave San Jose School and move on. I had just bought a house in the High Desert, and it was more than a few miles away. Before leaving for the desert I took an assignment that was offered me for summer school. The new school was a couple of miles up the road from the old San Jose School. The new school was called Fairview Elementary. I would have very young mentally handicapped students that were integrated into regular schools. Integration of handicapped kids into regular schools was sort of a new thing. Most schools were like San Jose, all handicapped. I wasn't real comfortable with the really small ones.

I'm a tall person and I must have looked like a giant to them. Since I had moved to the high desert traveling was getting to be a real hassle. I was driving a 150 miles a day. I started looking for a position with a different county school system. Meanwhile I kept working at Fairview. I met my new aide or assistant. Her name was Winnie. I thought that was a bit funny being named Winnie but I didn't ask. She was an angel, though different than Mary she was an angel in her own heaven. She loved these small kids. She had a heart bigger than Texas. We got to know each other and would talk all the time when we took the kids to the play ground. She knew each student and she knew each students parents. I couldn't figure out why she needed me there. But we learned very quickly how each other works and made a great classroom in a few weeks. Winnie would be absent off and on and she sometimes didn't look well but she always worked hard and was a good teacher to me. I don't know why but I never got to know any of the students in this class. None of them didn't do anything any stranger than any of the other students had done up to this point. None of them became close to me like in the other classes. Funny how some students click to you and latch on. Its funny how some things that seem so unimportant become so significant to your memory over time.

Good news from the high desert. The school I applied to for a position at wanted me like yesterday. Seems there was a shortage of Severally Handicapped teachers everywhere, especially men. I was only at Fairveiw for 4 months and had to leave as I took the position. It was only two miles from my new house. I was hesitant because I had nothing but good experiences, sometimes difficult but always good. I told Winnie about the move and she was not real happy that I was leaving but she was genuinely happy for me. I worked the rest of the summer with Winnie. She seemed to be missing more days now. Winnie and I said our good byes at the end of summer school 1984 and I was off to a new job, new house and a new life.

Chapter 19
New Class

The new school was much like the development center at San Jose School. Walking thru, it was evident that the students were of the lowest mentally capable and there was the same underlying oder of urine and diaper pails. As much as they tried that was something that would never go away. I would be on probation my first two years before I received my tenure. I was very watchful and mindful of everything I did or said. I was being escorted by the lead teacher to my new class and the assistant I would work with. I was told that I was there just to observe the first day and to watch and see how things were done. I think they were giving me the chance to change my mind. The class was very disabled, most in the worst way. There were some students with disfigurements and some with paralysis, some with both. All were extremely mentally disabled. All had to be hand fed and in most cases had to have their food pureed. All had to have diapers changed. My job in this class was to be a nurse and caretaker. It didn't seem like a school per sie but we did what we could to make the students comfortable. Part of our job description was to give parents a break. Although most of the time the students didn't really understand why they were doing it, we would at least motor them thru activities. We included them in everything that we did in class to the ability that each student had. This class was more mentally disabled then the class I had at San Jose with Kenny, Mikey and Mimi, if that is possible. Eveything was routine and everyday seemed like every other.

One student we had was extra fragile. He was very thin and very small. He couldn't have weighed more than 40 lbs with his clothes on. Each day he seemed more quiet, and every day he appeared thinner. I had only worked there for a few weeks and this student who I will call "Joe" was new also. Neither me nor my assistant knew him very well, nor had either one of us ever have talked to the parent. When feeding him he would spit up and it was difficult keeping any food down. Joe would not take liquids at all and we were becoming very concerned as Joe was becoming more and more lethargic. I tried to contact the parent with no luck. I told the principle and she had no luck calling. The following day I was going to have the school nurse take a look at him, maybe make a report or even a home visit. Joe was laying on a padded chair that had a rocker attached. It was low to the ground and blankets and tons of padding. He lay there early in the morning. He didn't move much except for his head rolled from side to side occasionally. As I was sitting by him with another small child in my hands and watching Joe, Joe went totally limp His arms fell to floor and his head did not move. I put the small child on the floor on a blanket and picked Joe up. He was lifeless. I listened to his heart and there was no beat. I yelled out to my assistant to call 911. She ran to the phone and called. She called the principle to come to the classroom. We started CPR and he immediately came back. He started breathing, ever so shallow but he was back. With in seconds it seems the fire department and paramedics were there and took over. We would not see him again. Joe lived for about a week and later died of some type of toxic poisoning. There was an investigation of his death. His mother it seems never fed him or at least rarely. Joe died of malnutrition and a toxic reaction to not being fed. Although we only heard very little of what happened to Joes mother we did hear she was arrested.

The very next day I would receive some very bad news. I had just gotten to work and I got a phone call. Marys husband called me and told me Mary had died. She had a heart attack in the classroom. They took her to the hospital where she was already dead. Now Mary was truly an angel, she was one person I knew that had earned her wings.

It was a tough week, student dies or for my money, murdered. My most favorite person dies, Mary. I got new students off and on for the next few months. I got the mayors son, he had M.S. He was very physically and mentally disabled. For the most part the months went by uneventful, until the day I got another call.

Winnies husband called my house and my wife called me at work to tell me she had died. I was feeling like I was a curse. My assistant Maureen was starting to feel uneasy. But Winnie too earned her wings. She had liver cancer. She never told anyone, She did not even tell a Doctor. Her husband told me she was embarrassed to see a doctor. The biggest regrets I have to this day is that I did not go Marys or Winnies funeral. I don't know why. If I could change things I would have gone. Some mistakes just cant be changed. I would remember them forever, for the things they did for me, but mostly for the things they did for my kids in the class. I will remember them for their true hearts.

Chapter 20
New Class Again: Toby

For the most part teachers in special education tried to change classes to those students with the least mental problems and more abilities. That isn't always true but I felt I put my time in with the most handicapped. There was an opening at the sister school that was about a half mile away, Ruth Sumney School. There were four classes all at a much higher abilitiy level than the development center I was working at before. It was a simple matter of asking and it was done. I had worked at the development center for nearly three years by this time and I was ready. My new class was very capable. We did things like the regular classes did, math, reading, writing. All of the work we did was at a much lower level than the regular class but you could see the growth in them. We had our problems though and one of them was Toby. He was always a match waiting to be a forrest fire. Toby had a shunt in his brain which allowed fluid that would build up to go to his stomach. Toby was our most capable but most volatile student. One minute he would be doing his addition using a calculator and the next throwing his art work paint and everything at me or the help.Toby and I would have many run ins. His favorite thing was to swing on the playground. Once on the swing he was impossible to get off. For awhile we would not allow him on the swing then we started to use it as a reward for good behavior. Toby wore a helmet since he would have very occasional seizures from his shunt not working just right. He fell alot. He had chipped teeth and scars on his chin and forehead. The helmet didn't always protect him. It seemed like we were calling his parents at least once a month to go get stitches. Toby didn't seem to mind. Toby sort of just fit into the class. He had his moments but so did the rest of the students in this class. (More to come on Toby).

Chapter 21
Mitchel (2)

As was part of the usuall procedure or progression of the year we would get new students. We would gain some and loose some. There was a big turn over. We had a lot of students from the airforce base which was close by. The Airmen would get restationed and off went our student. That happened a lot. I was told I was getting a new student within the week and I was anxiously anticipating him. I knew nothing about him. More often than not I would receive little to no paper work with the student to at least give a breif idea what the student was like so you had to do the best with what you had. Mitchel arrived. He was a very tall and slender student. He had jet black hair and teeth, boy did he have teeth. He was nearly as tall as I was. It was not long that he showed his true side. He had bad behavior, just like an off and on switch. Mitchel was much bigger than the other students and I was worried that he could hurt someone, including me. There was no distinction of behaviors in classes like mine. We had to deal with it the best we could. Sometimes we would just separate the student from the rest as best we could and get along with our class. When things looked like it would get really ugly we sent all the students out to play and I would deal with the aggressive behavior one on one. There was a small computer lab located inside the building we were in and I found with Mitchel I could get him calmed down by allowing him to play games. Whatever works! I would have to stay with him and monitor him while he was there and that took away from the rest of the class. I didn't take him there often but it was the one thing that would get him under control. At one time in the class he picked up a chair and threw it. On a particularly bad day he came in ready for battle. There seemed like nothing was controlling him. I worked him into the computer lab away from the other students and staff. He was my student so I had to deal with it. Mitchels thing was to bite himself. He would yell and scream and bite himself. He had a lot of scar tissue on his wrists where he would bite and tear. I got him seated by a computer which was a hand me down. He couldn't hurt it. I got a game going and it seemed to bring him down a level. He was still getting angry and aggressive but he was sitting and minding his business. I kept my distance at the same time keeping a close eye on him. He was showing extraordinary bizarre behavior. I kept notes on everything that happened. I learned early on to document everything. I turned to get my note book that I put down by a computer.

As I turned and with in one motion Mitchel got up ran to me and bit me in the shoulder as hard as he could. He stepped back and picked up the computer he was working at and aimlessly tossed it at me. I knew I was in trouble. He picked up a chair and threw that next. The teacher in the class next to me had his own problem children, but he came running in. The lab was a disaster. Mitchel had not finished and was still throwing broken pieces of computer. The other teacher and I looked at each other and saw no other choice. We grabbed him and wrestled him to the carpet. He was screaming and bitting his wrist all the way down. Another teacher had already called the principle John. He was on his way. He was out of the building for a meeting. John stepped in the lab. You could see the holy smoke look on his face. John called the father to come and get Mitchel. That was standard operating procerdure when things got totally out of hand. Dad came about an hour later and the other teacher and I had restrained him for the entire time. When Mitchels father stepped in, Mitchel went limp and it was like he was saying uh oh! We let him up. Mitchel went out the door with his Dad and he turned and looked at me, a glare that could kill. It was at that exact moment that I realized I knew Mitchel from years before, at the mental institution. It was the same Mitchel who about seven years before had bitten me in the same shoulder in the same place. I Have no scars to prove it but the irony of it all. Mitchel would be back and for the next year and a half he would haunt me. He had my number but he was more careful. He never again took me to the limit of restraining him. I think his Dad took care of that. Later at the end of Mitchels tenure with me, his father passed away. Mitchel was never the same. For the remainding months he was more sedate and sometimes even happy.

Chapter 22
Twins:
Dave and Danny

At one time, as teachers we were to make home visits to students houses. This was supposed to give us a better perspective of their home life and maybe some ideas on how we were to teach them in class. I had already done some visits and for the most part they were uneventful and "normal", except for the time I went to Kimberlys house and her dad offered a beer. More like he insisted. So we sat and drank beers for a few hours until it was time to leave. That visit was more like the kind of visit I liked. It was when I was scheduled to make a visit to the twins place is when I had a lot of surprises to come. They weren't actually twins, they were a year apart but they certainly passed for twins and everybody at the school called them twins.

The visits were all prearranged so they

knew we (I) was coming. Many of the students lived in rural areas and were sometimes a little hard to find. The twins house was no different and even more so. I started out after school and the map I had did not do it justice. I went from a nice asphalt road to a country graded road to what looked like an old wagon train, rutted out trail. The street signs were hand painted boards stuck in the ground. After an hour or so of driving I spotted his house. It was a very old mobile home, small but big enough. Before I could get to the house I had to pass thru a ten foot barbed wire fence which surrounded five acres of dirt and the house exactly in the middle. The fence was tall. It looked like a high security prison fence. Each pole had a goat skull on top of it, with skulls linning the bottom of each pole. Rattle snake skins were tacked in spirals around each pole with snake heads nailed randomly, like Christmas ornaments on every pole. I had to honk my horn to get in. The twins father came out unlocked the gate and as I drove in he relocked it. Their father was right out of Arkansas, with a southern draw. He was a nice enough guy, he welcomed me to his house. When I went in there was a very large pistol, revolver hanging on a coat rack. It was obviously loaded. Next to the coat rack were two shotguns, one was a new pump and the other was a double barrel that looked like it came from an antique collection. They also were loaded. The two boys who did not talk much were sitting on their bed which was also in the family room of the trailer. Me and the Father talked for a bit about school and life out in the middle of nowhere. He told me that he liked it that way and didn't like being bothered by people but understood that I had to make my visit. The boys mother came in from the small master bedroom. She was wearing a peasent dress and and high neck blouse. It was almost 100 degrees outside and they had no air conditioning. The boys mother said hi ,and that was about it for her part of the conversation. She sat the rest of the time quietly listening. I was there for about a half an hour and from the long drive to their house and way too much coffee I had to GO!

I asked if I could use the restroom and "he" pointed the direction. I went into the bathroom and saw that it was extremely small. I lifted the toilet lid and also saw that the toilet either didn't flush or wasn't flushed for what looked like days. I also found out by turning on the water in the sink that there wasn't any. So I peed in the sink as there was not one bit of room in the toilet. I put the lid down and went back to the family room. Their father was waiting for me right outside the door and asked me very hurridly " You didn't flush the toilet did you?" He forgot to tell me they only flush once a week as they did not have running water in the trailer. They had to bucket water in to the bathroom for the weekly flush. We had a nice talk about Arkansas and then I needed to leave as an hour or so is what our visits were to last. We shook hands goodbye,he unlocked the gate and I was on my way.

The next day I talked to another teacher who had the twins before me. She told me that their family was not poor, just the opposite. Their father had hundreds of thousands of dollars but preferred to live in near seclusion.

Chapter 23
Mork

Yes that is his real name, Mork. He was one of the happiest students that I would ever have. It didn't seem fair to be so happy and have the problems he had. Mork has the corner on shaking hands. If you let him he would shake your hand clean off. I use the word "has" because I just saw him and his parents the other day in town. Mork pops up all the time and I see him at least once a week. There was a time here that I didn't see him for about three years. And just the other day in the bowling alley Mork came up to me and started shaking my hand. His mother came up and told him "that's enough"! Morks parents made everything so much better for me during my early years in the high desert. They have a real perspective of their child. Mork of course tried to shake my hand again and his mom warned him not to do it again. Once is enough. Mork knew my name. After three years he still knew my name. He has an unerasable memory. I was so happy to see him. Maybe I was happier to see him then he was me. Mork was never my student,rather I knew him from school and would only had minimum contact with him until I got involved with a ranch that gave theraputic rides on horses. Morks parents are the ones who introduced me to it, and for several years I would go on weekends and help. I found out that many of the students in classes around the desert participated with the horse ranch. The Lady "B" ranch was my weekend escape. When the students got on a horse they were different people. They paid attention, if for no other reason they might fall off, but there was a sense about them that when they were on a horse they were something else. Mork was the ranches most faithful client. Mork was proud of himself when he was sitting tall on a 16 hand thouroughbred trained to give rides to the handicapped. I am sure I will see Mork tomorrow night as it is bowling night. Mork bowls in a league designed for handicapped individuals and my league is right after his. For now I see Mork and his parents at least once a week unless I see him in Walmart which has happened on more than one occaision. Mork is the kind of young man that you have to meet to believe him, and would hope that everyone could.

About two years after writing this Mork passed away.

Chapter 24
Megan

Each student is an individual with their own little quirks, clicks and whims. Each student wether they are mentally handicapped or an honor student with straight A's are all unique. Moodiness is something that even the most handicapped share with the most billiant. Megan a student who was very slight, skinny and at average height. She had many freckles with red hair. Megan had the same physical problem Kami had, tubular sclerosis. I don't know the details of her disease but it wasn't good. Kami had it where it was fatal. Megan had it where it seemed to be mostly on her face and head. Megan was like a lot of the students that I had. She played with her fingers and rocked back and forth. She would throw her crayons and paper, she didn't like to touch objects or people for that matter. She treated people like objects . Megan had a very difficult time holding hands when she needed to;when we took little mini field trips to the store or just on walks. One day she came on the bus like any other day, but she was screaming at the top of her voice. She never talked, never uttered a word. She was screaming so loud I could hear her from the bus stop before the bus even came to a stop. I got her out of the bus thinking it was something that upset her on the bus. We took her and the rest of the class into the classroom where she continued screaming. This wasn't your everyday run of the mill scream. It was a shrieking, horror movie scream. For two hours she screamed and screamed and screamed. Our class was an open class here just like the one at San Jose school. Every class could hear the volumous screech. There was nothing else to be heard. Her scream drowned out everything else at the school and it did not cease. I had already called her dad who was a single parent like many of our parents of special kids were. He told me she started screaming the night before for no appeerent reason. He was hoping by going to school she would quit. It didn't quit but got much worse. We just had to deal with it. Megan would clinch her fists and tighten her arms and scream as loud as her pair of lungs would allow her to. By the end of that day she was still screaming and she only stopped during lunch, just long enough to get food in her mouth. When she got on the bus to go home she was still screaming. I could hear her as the bus made its way down the block. I talked to her dad again and he said he would take her to the doctor.

The following day Megan came with a note. The doctor said there was nothing wrong with her that was appeerent. When Megan came that same day she was still screaming and as far as her dad and I could tell she had been screaming for the past 72 hours. This was Tuesday, and she hadn't stopped screaming, Friday still going at it and hadn't stopped all week. One solid week Megan had not stopped screaming. It was very warrying on us all at the school but it was the kind of thing to expect, never trained for, just expect the unexpected. The following week after a very quiet week end at home I came to work almost forgetting the Megan screaming, but as I sat outside the school waiting for the busses to arrive I could hear her coming from up the street. I could hear her while she was on the bus, windows closed. The bus pulled up in the bus circle and Megan was already standing up screaming waiting to get off. Dad also told me that she has not stopped over the weekend. She only took time to breath and eat. Megan slept only a couple of hours over the weekend. Her face was red and her veins were visible in her fore head from pushing so hard on her lungs. The entire week went by with Megan screaming without end. It was wearing our patience thin at the school and it seemed that there was no cure for her desire to scream. It was like she was seeing a monster or a ghost. Her father had no explaination for her bizarre screaming but we were to have a weekend to think about it, to look forward to the loud, all present shrill.

Monday arrived and Megan showed up screaming once again. No solutions. Tuesday, screaming non stop. Wednesday, Megan was sitting at her desk screaming her head off, within one split millisecond, she stopped. She stopped screaming. She looked up and gave a somewhat simili of a smile and started rocking and fooling with her hands. It was utter quiet. A couple of other teachers came in to the room. They were wondering what was wrong. We were all so used to the screaming it was an everyday event and when she abruptly quit it was like we couldn't stand the quiet. It was almost as bizarre when she stopped screaming so suddenly as it was her screaming non stop. She just plain stopped, as fast as she started, she stopped. I called her father and he thought I was joking about her not screaming. He was being called a couple of times a day to try and solve Megans

problem. For the next year of Megan in my class she never screamed again. We will never know why she screamed or what was going through her mind.
Between Tommys' head banging and Megans screaming I don't know which was worse.

Chapter 25
Brandon

A small boy, very petite, frail but very bright. Brandon had no other handicapp other than he was very weak from a bad heart. He had a small hole in one of his ventricles or a malfunctioning valve. He was in our class with Tony and Megan. Brandon had good speech and would talk our heads off all the time. He was with us because he was looking to have surgery to get his heart fixed and we kept a close eye on him. He was too frail to go to regular classes at a regular school. He probably would have been better off there because it seemed like our students were always sick or just getting over from being sick. Brandon was very susceptible to getting ill and he was waiting in our class so he would be ready for his upcoming operation. Brandon was a lot like Miky. He clung to me all the time. He followed me around and talked to me constantly. We had the most interesting conversations about his favorite toys and some of the programs he would watch on T.V.

After four months with Brandon I got to know his parents as good friends. They would even call me at home off and on just to talk about Brandon and how he looked at school, they would ask, was he coughing? Did he play much? We had to watch how much he exerted himself.Brandon always wanted to do more than his little heart was able. You could tell he had so much energy stored up in his mind but his poor frail body kept telling him he couldn't do it. He would breath hard just from going from the class to the out door pic nic bench which was right outside the door. Brandon hung in there and did everything he could, and a little more.

Brandons mother called me in the afternoon and said that he needed to go to surgery that next day. The hospital had an opening and he was feeling as well as he could considering his problem. He checked in the hospital early in the week, Monday or Tuesday as I remember. The surgery was to be one that the doctors at the hospital do routinely and Brandon would be there at the hospital for a couple of weeks. I was looking forward to getting him back in class so he could recooperate and then he was going to go to regular classes at the school next door to us. I expected a call the next day after his operation to see how everything went.

I got to work extra early every morning. This morning was no different. We always get things prepared for the day, art activities, reading or language lessons. We tried to do something a little different every day just to keep the students on their toes. Besides I know I knew I needed a breather before they came to school on the bus. I wasn't so eager when Megan was coming to school screaming. I grabbed a cup of coffee and a couple of donuts at the coffee shop. When the class was done being set up I would sit in the teachers lounge where I could see the buses pull up from the nice picture window. I was sitting talking to one of the other four teachers at the school as she would get there early too. When the phone rang I suspected it was Brandons' mother as she said she would call first thing in the morning. Brandon had his surgery late at night. When I picked up the phone the voice on the other side was barely a faint whisper, but it was brandons mother as I still recognized her voice. She said "we lost Brandon". I asked her what she meant. She repeated herself, and went on to tell me he died on the operating table. His little heart could not take the operation. Little Brandon barely 60 pounds was dead.

I don't like funerals or Graveyards. Who

does? But Brandon was very special and a brave kid. He knew that he was very sick. I went to the short but very large funeral. There were a lot of people there. I went in the procession and arrived at Rose Hills Cemetary where he was to be buried. I parked nearly a quarter of a mile away. There were that many people. What was sad but still happy at the same time was that the cemetery had a large site set aside for young kids. Before each headstone were stuffed animals, and pinwheels, and toys that were left by family members and friends. Brandons grave was covered with toys and pin wheels. There was not enough words for me to explain to Brandons mother how sorry I was and that we really lost a good kid. But I looked around the two acre childrens cemetery and saw that there were hundreds of others and I slipped away and went home. I felt a little guilty about leaving so abruptly. It was my way of dealing with that kind of tradgedy. At this point I had already lost 9 students. I found something out about myself. I don't deal well with the death of a student or of my assistants.

Chapter 26
"Little Hitler"

All of the principals I have worked with have been good hard working people. Some of them have been almost invisible but they did a good job and they were always there to help out. People like Martha Smith were one of a kind. Bill as I will call him was quite another story. Bill earned a name, a moniker, " Little Hitler". He was the epitamy of the non communicater, he was the person who you were watching behind your back. When Mitchel was trashing the computers he was the one who would not help. He stayed in his little office plotting how best to disrupt your day and how best to make you look bad. He had no skills as a leader what so ever.

By the time he became the principal I had worked at Sumney school for a few months and moved on to a class on a regular campus with high functioning students who were able to get along with the general public. These students were hand picked and they never did anything that was weird or bizarre. Bill on the other hand made my days miserable. It wasn't just me but most of the teachers that worked under him were either terrified or psychologically brutalized. He would be one of the reasons I left the county classes eventually.

When he got the name Little Hitler I don't know, and who gave it to him? I don't know that either. I just know he deserved it. He made teaching a living hell. He was an incompitent human being much less a principal.

I am not a quiter, but I found that this was an excellent opportunity or justification, in my mind anyway to put the teachers hat away for awhile and take a review where I was and where I was going with teaching. If this was the way it was going to be the rest of my career then I wanted nothing to do with it. I decided to take a rest. I turned in my resignation in the middle of the year of 1988. I had no job offers and had no income but yet I felt that in my heart this was the right thing to do. After the first month of sitting around the house and living off of my savings I was really missing being with the students. I had already taken out most of my retirement. I was going to be broke if I didn't start looking. It didn't take me two days to find a position back with the old school district in L.A. County. This wasn't going to be like the old class with the mentally retarded kids it was going to be much different. These students were those "bad" kids that nobody wanted. Bad behaviors and bad attitudes. I wouldn't start for a few months but I knew I had a job there.

Bill was still causing problems with the teachers that chose to stay and fight it out but I know I did the right thing. Bill didn't know it but he was actually on his way out. He had received many complaints from teachers and parents. One day he just wasn't there anymore. He disappeared. Gone. Come to find out after about a year or so what happened to him. As the cliché goes " He rose to his highest level of incompetence" He was let go from his position but he went on to be a superintendent of a small school district up north of here...way up north. I hope they are happy with him as he was a thorn in our side.

As bad as he was (Bill) he was still responsible for being a factor in a positive change in my career. My retirement savings was all gone by then but it was worth it.

Chapter 27
Maria

After months of waiting to get to my new job I finally started. I knew the principal some and I knew she was the real deal. I knew her from some of the meetings I went to when I worked at San Jose School. Trudy was a concerned principal and she would help you in any way she could but her first priority were the students. She took time the first day to show me around and just hang out and watch how things were done. My class hadn't actually been formed yet and I had a few days to get organized. She was another exceptional principal.

I used my preparation days to read the student profiles and records before I actually got them in class. It wasn't a pretty site. Some of them had committed violent crimes. Some of them had anti social behavior, drugs, fighting, you name it, I had them all. One thing they all had in common was they were all smart. They weren't mentally deficient or retarded. These were students that other than their attitude problems could otherwise be the cream of the crop.

Monday came and the students got off of the bus, and straight to class. Most were on probation through the legal system so they did what they were told as there was only one other place they could go and that was lock up, juvenile hall. Everday was another fight to break up, or scuffle. We were trained to break up fights without getting hurt ourselves and after time dealing with all of their personal problems and baggage was just part of the normal routine. I had one girl in my class and her name was Marie. She was absent a lot but when she was there she did her work and rarely got into it with the other students. She was not one to back down from a fight. But she did avoid them. As I remember she did have a couple of combats, always with boys from the other classrooms. There were other girls in the school but she had little to do with them. Maria was a foster child and had her battles with her parents. I would get daily reports from them how she was doing at home and I would return favor by telling them how she was doing here.

Maria one day did not come to school anymore. She was placed in another foster home on the other side of town and she would eventually go to another school like this one. There were a lot of schools like this for troubled or problem kids. Still the days went on breaking up fights half the time and teaching the other. One day a student from another class brought a sawed off shot gun on the bus with the purpose in mind to shoot the teacher. Luckily the bus driver saw it hidden under his pants and the police were notified somehow. He never made it to school. I am sure he served a lot of time in lock up for that.

I had a long trip everyday, over 80 miles each way. I liked the job enough to make the trip. I would stop and get two cups of coffee for the trip there and a big soda for the trip back. When I got home I liked to take a breather from breaking up fights and the long drive home.I liked to kick back for a few minutes and watch the news, have a snack and wind down. I was watching the 4 oclck news and there was a report of a Taxi being robbed and the driver was shot and killed. The culprits as it was reported were three young ladys and they got away with 20 dollars. I thought it was pitiful. Our news is filled with that kind of stuff. As the news report went the story continued and ther was a rather crude artist rendition of the three that robbed the Taxi. One picture looked familiar but it wasn't a real good picture. It looked like a lot of people I've met over the years.

I got very tired on work days and would go to bed early for the long drive to work. Before bed I flipped the news on again. There was a sort of special report. The police had caught the three young women who killed the taxi driver and there was a live camera. The three young women were being escorted into the police station. They passed by the camera one by one, handcuffed and trying to hide their faces. As the last girl went by she looked up straight at the T.V. It was Maria. I hadn't seen her for months but I recognized her as though I had her in my class yesterday. Now I can tell the similarity to the drawing that I didn't quite identify. It was her. She was 17 years old, but she was being jailed and cuffed like an adult. She like many of the students I had over the years would disappear from my class but not my memory.

Chapter 28
Paulson

Paulson reminded me of Brandon in his appearance. Paulson was small and somewhat fragile looking but that is where it stopped. Paulson was a violent, destructive, plotting little bomb. He was a match in a gas tank. He had gotten in several fights over the time I was there and he didn't care if they were boys or girls, or three times his size. If he thought they were picking on him or said something he didn't like his flame would rise instantly. He would explode. We spent many days restraining Paulson physically. His size did not matter. As small as he was he could still lift three grown men off of the ground when sitting right on him. On the other side of things he could be the nicest well behaved boy you ever met. Paulson was unpredictable at best. On his good days Paulson was allowed to help in a classroom in a large building just a hudred feet or so from our "bunker".

These classes were totally separate from ours and had to go through two locked gates to get there. Most of the students there were very low functioning and much like the kids I had at the first teaching job I had. When Paulson was good he got to go and when he was bad he didn't. Paulson was a very good helper on a good day. I am not sure what he was asked to do by the teacher in the class that he was helping in but he didn't want to do it. He started to get mad at the teacher and was asked to go back to the class in our building. Paulson didn't want to go and he had to be escorted by two of us as he was screaming obsenities and being beligerant. As he was being escorted he yelled out that he was going to burn the place down along with "F#@% and "S&%# and just about every letter in the alphabet. We were able to control him by the time he got inside the classroom. He was still angry but he did his work and finished his assignments. It was a Friday so he was probably figuring that he didn't want to get into any big trouble before the week end.

By the time the buses came and picked him and the rest of the class up he was in perfect behavior. Long day over and got in my car for the long drive home. It really wasn't a bad day even considering the little problem with Paulson. Sometimes the weekends were crazier than the days at work with the students that I had. Sometimes I couldn't wait for Monday. I started liking the drive to a from work. It was the only peace and quiet I would get many times.

Monday morning came and I got my two coffees and turned the radio on to my favorite talk show. It took me at least an hour, sometimes hour and fifteen minutes to get to work, and I wasn't a slow driver. I pulled into the street that the school was on and noticed a couple of red trucks parked outside the building that Paulson helped in. I got out of my car to find out there was no school today as Paulson had burned down the classrooms that he worked in. Actually he didn't burn them down. He cleverly snuck in on Sunday night and torched the insides. All the furniture, toys and papers were strun all around the play ground where the firemen had put it. The teacher of the class told the admin that Paulson had said what he said but they didn't take his threat seriously. Paulson was arrested and there was plenty of prooof he did it, shoe prints, finger prints and the fact he came to school Monday morning in the same clothes he was wearing when he strated the fire. He smelled of smoke. He seemed to be just waiting around to get arrested. They cuffed him and took him away, probably to juvenile hall. We were given the choice to go home or put in a days work while both parts of the school were closed for the day. I chose to stay for the day and help clean up some of the mess from the fire. Paulson burned out half the severelly handicapped school rooms, but it smeeled throughout. It took an entire week to repair and desmell everything. The students that were supposed be using that building were put at a different school temporarily.

Paulson never came back. He was assigned a therapist to help him with his problems. He was in lock up for a long time or at least until the time I had resigned my position, which wasn't till after the upcoming summer. The drive was getting to me and it was wearing on my car. I didn't think that it would last much longer so I had started looking for something a little closer. It wasn't long till I found a school district close by that had an opening for special ed. I went to talk with the principal at Hook Jr High, in Victorville. I went to just talk to him and look at the school. He hired me on the spot. It seems there was a big shortage of special ed teachers in the area of severally handicapped. Again it didn't hurt being a male as there were even fewer of us. It was really odd getting hired so quickly, and with almost no interveiw at all. This class evidentally was open for a new teacher for a couple of years. I was happy to take it site unseen. I couldn't wait. I had a whole summer to finish off in Lancaster with the tough kids. Few kids turned up to school that summer and it was easy. Working there was exciting and character revealing but my stay there was also very anti climatic. One day there and the next day not.

Chapter 29
The New School: (Hook Jr.) Saul

It was the first day of school at Hook Jr. and before class even arrived there were circumstances. This school had never had these kind of kids before as I found out after the fact. They had not one clue what they were in for. There was not a plan or a fore thought about the daily routine or the special needs these students would need. When I got to my room which I hadn't seen yet, I noticed it was a regular classroom cut in half. After all we were just a handicapped class and we wouldn't need regular facilities. They were wrong of course. We actually needed twice the room as we were to get two wheelchair students. Those things eventually worked themselves out but that took months not days. We eventually moved into a regular class when one opened up, but not before I met my class to be. Saul was my first student. He was tall,thin and sad eyed. A stiff breeze could knock him over. Saul would talk, talk, talk, talk. He had a temper and could get very angry at his classmates if it got too noisy or if they teased him. He didn't get mad very often and when he did it didn't take much to calm him down. Paul walked to school by himself as he lived right around the corner from the school. I was always worried about that but it was his parents choice and they spent weeks before school started showing him how to get there and what to do if there were a problem. We always kept an eye open for Saul, especially if he was late. One day he was really late and we couldn't get a hold of his parents right away. Usually they would call us if he wasn't going to be there for a Dr. appointment or whatever. The fact is Saul was rarely absent. We tried and tried to get a hold of his parents because he wasn't there after an hour and a half. It wasn't long after that though that his parents were contacted and found. They were out shopping. Sauls Dad told me he should have been there and became very worried. His Dad said that they had an argument that morning about something and Paul said he was going to run away. Sauls father called the police and they immediately started looking for him. Saul knew where he was going and how he was going to get there but the only way he knew the direction was to follow the freeway. That would take him to his old house. It was only about a half an hour till the highway patrol spotted him. Saul was walking down the middle barrier of a major freeway. He wasn't walking down the side but right down the middle. He had to have crossed three lanes of busy freeway traffic to get to the middle. The Highway Patrol picked him up and brought him home. They had to close down the freeway for a few minutes so just in case he would run off he wouldn't get hurt. The freeway was a mess as it was in the newspaper the next day.

Saul was driven to school the next day by his father. Saul talked about his little excursion as though he was proud of it, and for the weeks after that is all he talked about. The following year at Hook Jr. Sauls' younger brother attended and kept a better watch on him and he was allowed to walk to school once again.

Chapter 30
Lora

We had moved into our new class and it was three times the size of the old one. Our new class was a portable but it had all of the amenities, a sink, real carpet and chalk boards. By the time we got the new class room we were slowly getting more students and loosing some to other programs. Things were changing, we could actually run lessons and do activities. We went on walks, did our own P.E. activities and class was actually fun. I worked with good people and think me and the principal at the time had a good understanding. I did my thing and he did his. I knew my job and I knew it well. Slowly more new students came to us. Our room was filling up. Lora was one of the new students this year. I knew her a bit as she was a student at the same school Brandon was in but I rarely had any contact with her. I also knew here from the theraputic horse ranch I would go to once in awhile being they were part of the special Olympics which I was heavily involved with but that is a whole other book. I had little to do with here either, and we would have to make friends and aquantinces in the new classroom. She was a thin blonde full of energy autistic teenager. Lora was another student that loved to wave her fingers in front of her eyes. She got some kind of stimulation from it, who knows? She too had an insatiable appetite. You had to watch your food in this class. Coffeee, sodas, anything that looked edible was fair game for her and she would take it in a heartbeat. She even tried to take food right from my hand. Lora had a few bad habits. She was like the boy on the swing, she didn't like clothes. A few weeks had gone by and little by little Lora became more comfortable about her environment, and Lora had started throwing off clothes. Out of nowhere Sara would walk through the classroom and throw a blouse off or her shoes. It wasn't real serious, it was just once in awhile, but very unpredictable. Other little habits started surfacing. Lora would stand by the class door and play with the door knob. She was fascinated by it. It made a little squeek and click and she would play with it over and over. As much as we tried we had a very difficult time keeping her in her seat. Over a few months with Lora it was getting worse as time went on. Lora was starting to run out of class and we would have to chase her down. She was very sneaky and quiet. She would go to the door knob and play around with it. Before we knew it she was out the class running down the halls. Sometimes she would run out and start taking her clothes off. We always caught her before she got to far or too many articles of clothing off.

Lora was really getting to test our nerves and it seemed like no matter what we did she do do everything she could to escape. Food became unimportant. Her goal was to get out of class and she was getting better at it. On this day it was very noisy in the class. We were doing a little project with music going and the students were all out of their desks. One small group was dancing and the other group was doing some kind of art project. Lora had other ideas. I had one assistant in my class so it was relatively difficult to keep all the kids busy and occupied. My assistant looked up and around and asked me "where is Lora"? I looked up and around and did not see her in class. I ran outside but this time I did not see her running off in her usuall direction, I didn't see her at all. I ran back in the classroom to call the office to put out an all points on her. I called the office and they sent out the campus security for her.

When I went to the back of the room where there is a picture window that looks out to the park soccer field with a fence between our room and the field, There I saw Lora standing at the fence, right in front of our class back window with not one stitch of clothing on. She was bare butt naked. Of course all of the other classes that faced the soccer field could see her too.

I grabbed a blanket from the sofa in our class, opened the back window, hopped throught the window and over the fence. I wrapped her up with the blanket and walked her back around the field and through a gate that was on he other side of school. Me and my assistant took a totally different look on how to control Lora and how we would not let her get away without locking the door inside,which by the way we would not be allowed to do anyway. We put a bell on the door that would ring when opened. It was irritating but she had a very difficult time getting out without us knowing. Lora had escaped several times since the soccer field incident but we always caught her before she could disrobe or get very far. Lora stayed with us for a few years at Hook Jr. High School. She was only one of our challenges. She made the class interesting and she kept me well exercised, I always got a good run in when Lora was at school.

Chapter 31
Lati

Lati was a very large Samoan girl. She was at least 5' 11" and she was big, very large. She always without fail came to school with her hair done in two little buns and they were never even. As large as she was she had a high pitch squeaky voice. I had a chance to read her profile and immense amount of records that were accumulated over her 16 years. She had a file a foot thick.

It took me at least two hours to read her files. Many times I didn't get files or records until weeks after the student actually came in my room. I was very lucky with Lati and got her entire full portfolio weeks before she enrolled. Her records were the epitimy of documentation but they didn't prepare me for the reality and actuality of who she was and things she could do.

Lati never ceased to amaze us. If it was written down she could write it and if it was written down she would not forget it. All we had to do is tell her once and she would not forget. I found real quick though that when she was instructed for instance to write your name; she would keep writing it over and over she would write her name all day long if she wasn't told to stop. I had to be very specific on what her assignment was or what I wanted her to do. Often our class would take turns at the blackboard and write our name or some of the new words for that day. Lienati had beautiful cursive hand writng. Her hand writing on the board went way beyond what one could possibly believe unless you could see it. Otherwise you had to be there. We would write a sentence or two on the blackboard and the students would take turns coping it to practice doing board work. Lienati copied the sentences. I didn't have the greatest handwriting. Lienati copied exactly what I wrote on the board. She copied it so exact that even the slightest fluctuation in my writing was mirrored. Lienati had no actual style of her own. She would only do what others did and she did it near exactly. I tried to get her to write words when I told her the word and she could not do it. What she could do was to cursively write a word backwards, exactly backwards from something copied from the board, exactly backwards. If you asked her to she could copy anything written on the board, upside down and backwards. The amazing thing was that even upside down and backwards the same fluctuations of style were still made but in reverse. This was not the only ability she had. She could draw anything that put before here. Given the time she could reproduce a drawing or picture, like it was a photo. She had a favorite picture she must have had imprinted on her mind. She could draw a certain horse drawing, it looked like my little pony. It was always the same. Alittle smaller a little bigger sometimes but it was always the same.

Lati could dance. She loved to dance but had only one step. Turn on the music and she would quietly mumble the words. Sitting or standing she had the beat. There are no words to describe Latis' dancing. It was a sight that only those privileged few would ever see, but picture a 5' 11" Samoan girl, over 400 lbs doing the mashed potato or the twist. I think the picture is clear. She was always happy and she always made us happy. Lati moved on to another school the following year. She was a foster child and she was autistic.

Chapter 32
Mickey (great guy)

Mickey was a great assistant. He cared about our students and it was easy to tell. He had never worked with handicapped students before but he dove right in and co-piloted the ship. If Mickey didn't something was right he would tell you and he would give a good practicle alternative. I took his advice many times. He always had sage wisdom although he did have some nutty ideas at least in my opinion. But that is what made Mickey such a great person to work with. He was much older then I was, and he had a work ethic that rubbed off on me.

Mickey would pic up a penny from the ground when he was on campus. He would tell me, 99 more and I have a dollar. I would get to work extra early so we would have coffee and time to talk about politics, sports, or anything controversial. At times others would join us, but mostly there were three, me, Mickey and Gene. Gene is another teacher of which I remained friends for years and to this day. Mickey worked with me through some of the hard times and I'm only sorry that I let him slip from my fingers, to another class, (later)

Chapter 33
Toby (Again)

Some students use your class like a revolving door. I had a lot of students that would be there one week and not the next, never see them again. Like Mike at the mental institution, almost seven years later and have him only to bite me again.

Toby was back! Remember Toby? He was the kid with the tube in his head to drain excess fluid to his stomach. Every once in awhile his shunt wouldn't work well. The valve would stick or something. Toby started having more seizures and other problems like passing out before he was scheduled to come to us at the regular Jr. High School. Toby had gone into surgery to fix the problem. He was to get a new shunt valve. When he came out of surgery he was blind. That of course did not stop him from coming to our class. It was weeks before he came to us though. He was getting mobility training at home. He learned how to use his white and red stick that all blind people carry around. He was learning the basics of how to read braille. Toby was a very capable student, he just had a terrible temper. He finally showed up to class and being blind did not soften his flammable personality.

After only a week or two at Hook Jr. Toby had almost every step on campus memorized. He did not like using his stick, it got in his way. It was a must though. He was required to use his stick especially when we went for a walk in the community. Toby was to have none of that. Everytime we went to lunch or did anything out side of class we made him take his stick but he would throw it and swing it at us. Toby had a sixth sense about his surroundings and where he was at all times. We could move the chairs around in the classroom and it seemed like he could still see. He would move around them and never touch them. In the class we didn't enforce the stick law. He used his hands very efficiently. When we went outside to lunch or to the park next door to the school he would carry his stick but he wouldn't use it. He folded the cane up and put it in his pocket. He was a sneaky little guy. Tobys' favorite thing was the walk to the park that we took nearly everyday when the weather was good. The park had climbing equipment, swings and moving bridges. Toby loved the swing. Although he was blind he knew when someone was one was on it. When he wanted the swing he would take his cane out and put it front of the student on the swing and try to block him. He would even sacrifice himself and get hit by the swinger, stopping him and pull him off of the swing. He had been hit so many times or fallen down that one more time on the kisser wouldn't bother him. It was worth it for the swing.

Toby was very quick to learn braille. Fred, my assistant in the classroom took a quick course in how to use the brailler. Toby was always just one step behind Fred. He could do math, reading and writing with braille, but when he didn't want to do his work he would bang on and push the brailler off of the table. When he got really mad Toby would get up and push chairs down and wipe the table clean from any other students work. He quite regularly would take his cane out and fling it around and scream at us that he wasn't going to work anymore till he got to swing at the park. We didn't bargain with him. Work first play later! Regardless our class eventually always made it to the park. Toby had great interest in the moving bridge. He had to cross it to get to the slide. The bridge was very wobbly. Toby was very careful with the expantion as no two steps were ever the same. We were at the small playground at the park when Toby decided to give the bridge a try. He had been on it many times but he was also wary of it. It was a challenge for him being that he could not memorize it, it was always unpredictable. Toby was nearly all the way across the bridge. He was by himself, he didn't need much help, not that he would of let us help him in the first place. He started taking his final step and the span seemed to move from right under his foot. He did a complete frontal endo. His chin hit the steal bar with a sharp corner that was hidden at the end of the bridge. He hit his chin with the full force of his fall. Blood splattered from his mouth and chin. It was all over the place and Tony acted like nothing was wrong. He got up quickly and said loudly, Why am I all wet? It was blood all over his clothes and all over the sand that filled the playground. He had a gash that was at least three inches wide at the very point of his chin and he had one chipped tooth, and of course soaked with blood. I ran to the park restroom and grabbed a wad of paper towels. The rest of the story: call dad, dad picks up, 20 stitches. It was like business as usual with Toby. His dad just asked how bad is it this time? Toby came back the next day. His chin was swelled up and his tooth chipped but I couldn't tell which one, he had so many.

Toby came in the class, and the first

thing he asked was when are we going to the park? I just told Tony, not for awhile.

Tobys' dad was in the Airforce and was being shipped out so that ment that he would be exiting my class soon. The Airforce base that was very close to our school was closing down and all of the Airmen would be leaving eventually. We lost almost half of our class that year and Toby was one of them. Unless I transferred to Germany I wouldn't be seeing Toby for a long time.

Chapter 34
Ronnie:
(Worlds biggest smile)

Some students didn't do weird or bizarre things. There were a few that just stood out because of who they are and just their presence in class made everything a little bit better. Ronnie was one of those kids. He was a small student who was wheelchair bound and could not talk. He was very quiet and would cry sometimes but very rarely. His muscles were extremely tight from his disease. He had Cereberal Palsy and his diagnosis was not good. Eventually he would succumb to his disorder but not while he was in my class. Our class would watch T.V. off and on and one day as we were watching the only channel we got in class a commercial came on. Several people came on the commercial, one after the other. Each were giving their testimony to the church they were advertising. The last testimonial came on and Ronnie straightened straight out in his wheelchair. He started laughing his head off. I wasn't watching the T.V. so I didn't know what was going on. I looked up at the television and there was Ronnies mom talking loud and happy with her church voice. Ronnie was histerical. I saw Ronnies mom everyday so I recognized her immediately. When donnies mom came to pick him up from school I told her of the T.V. appearance. When Ronnie saw his mom for the pick up he started laughing again. Every time we watched T.V. after that we always watched for his mother.

Ronnie had an interesting family. Although it was limited to him and his mother and a brother. Even though I talked to Ronnies Mom all the time she never mentioned a brother. One day as we were talking she mentioned it as just a second hand thought. Ronnies' brother was an Identical twin. Ronnie was 16 years old which would normally make him a high school student. Ronnie of course was bound to a wheel chair and several physical disabilities, he was very small weighing only 60-65 lbs. Ronnies brother as I was told by his Mom was 6'1" 180 lbs and was the school football and baseball star. He had everything going for him. When he got his drivers lisence Jonnie (Ronnies brother) would pick him up often after school. It must of felt odd for Jonnie looking at his brother who was "identical" but so different. Jonnie got into trouble at school alot and eventually fell out of sight. Ronnie went on to the high school program and got old enough to go on to things for students after they are done with their education. After he left our Jr. High school program I never saw him again nor his mother. I will remember that Ronnie had the biggest smile. When he wasn't smiling he was laughing.

Chapter 35
Willy

Willy was one of many students I had in class with me with Toby, Lati, Ronnie, Saul, etc, etc. He fit right in. Although he was much smaller in size, his temper and physical strength made up for any deficiencies. He was a cute little boy, very fair skin. He had a cowlick that always stuck straight up from the back of his hair, reminding me of Alfalfa on the little rascals. Willy was a little rascal. Most apparent was his eyes. They were so cross eyed it was amazing he could see anything. He had corrective glasses but he broke so many pairs he just stopped wearing them.

For his size Willy had great physical strength. We held his hands at all times when we went to the park, when we went to lunch, or anywhere. Once outside Willy would run from us trying to get ahead of the group. He liked to think he was the boss. Toby and Willy were mortal enemies.

For what ever reason they did not like each other. Although Toby was blind he knew when Willy was coming near him and they would fight, throw swings at each other, bite, kick, pull hair, you name it. If it wasn't so serious it would have been funny. Willy had a mouth on him. He knew every curse word and a few I have never heard. When Willy and Toby got into a skirmish, Willy would "F----n , **B----, GD,** SB, ….#%#@*&, and he was loud. All of the classes around us could hear him screaming at the top of his lungs. Tony would just scream in fear, no words attached. AS long as we kept them separated there wasn't a problem. Tony sat on one side of the room and Billy on the other. When Tony left with his Dad who was in the Air force to Germany. Willy seemed to miss him although they couldn't stand each other, for Willy it was obvious he missed his nemeses. For all of that, that is not why I wrote about Willy. His Father was much more interesting. Willy was late every day. He was never on time for school. His Father would bring him in and drop him off in the bus circle after all of the buses were gone. The bus circle was close enough to the classroom so I would get a glimpse of his Dads truck when he came in. But up to that time I could never catch him to talk to him. His truck was a broken down old ford 71-72 that smoked like a chimney and made so much noise that the other teachers around us had complained to the principal about the rattle and bangs it made when he pulled in to drop Willy off. He wouldn't stick around long enough for me to meet him. Usually teachers got to meet the parents before the student came to class but in this case Willy was signed up during the summer when I was off on vacation. I had a plan. I would go out to the bus circle and flag him down when he came screaming in, in his smoke mobile. I waited behind one of the portable classrooms that was right up to the bus circle. All the students had already gone to class and my assistants were watching them. I was determined to get to meet Willys Dad. I could hear the truck coming from way down the street. It pulled in the circle right in front of me in a cloud of smoke. Willy jumped out, almost looked like his Dad threw him out. I ran up to the passenger door before it could close and said " Hi I am Willys teacher. He looked just like Billy but a bigger version. He had crossed eyes and and a cowlick. Believe it or not, his name was Will. He had a deep Southern draw, filthy jeans and a red flannel shirt with a small tear on the right shoulder. With his almost Ozarkian voice he said "hey". Not hi but "hey". I could only think, Gommer, Gommer Pyle. He went on to say "I ben wait'n to meet cha".

He shut off his truck. He got out and told me he doesn't slow down or stop his truck because he cant get it started again, and he doesn't have a silence, "likes to get home in a hurry." After talking to him for a half hour or so he said he needed to go home and do some errands. He got in his truck, slammed the door. Like he said the truck wouldn't start again, and like Willy, he let out a few choice words. Willy picked up every finesse of the English language that his father had. I was not surprised. The truck not starting Bill just got out of his truck and walked off telling me he would be back for the truck in a short time. He kept walking off campus with me starring at this heap of a vehicle in the middle of the bus circle. I went to the classroom. It was still there five hours later. An hour more and the buses would be showing up to pick up the students and the truck was in the way or at least an obstacle to maneuver around. Just 15 minutes before the buses Willys Dad, Will showed up with a battery for the truck. I saw him from the classroom window. I went out to see if he needed help. He didn't know it but he did! When he opened the hood to the truck It was apparent how much help he did need. The entire engine was held together by duct tape, bailing wire, and faith. I don't know where he got the new battery. I didn't ask. Took the old battery out put it on the curb in front of the classroom I had hid behind. He slipped the new battery in, and when he did he went to the back of the truck for some duct tape and wound it around the battery bracket half a dozen times. I put the battery wires on for him. Buses were starting to pull in. Willy was outside with me so he could hopefully ride home with his Dad. Will and Willy were finally in the truck. Will turned the key. In a cloud of smoke, the truck started right up. He didn't wait a split second. He was off and running, out the bus circle and down the street. I could hear him a block away as he left. Given the option I would guess that Billy had more abilities then his father. Willy could read some but his father could not read one word nor do one bit of arithmetic.

Willy stayed with me for a couple of years. Our summer school was full of surprises. All the students go to summer school. Billy was no exception, but by that time we had talked Will to let his son ride the bus. It took six months for us to realize that he didn't understand that there were buses for the special kids. Our summer was spent almost entirely at the high school swimming pool. It was great. Eat snack, suits on, swim dry off, eat lunch, go home early. Willy had a problem. Once in the pool he did not like to get out. He would not get out for anything. There were almost two hundred kids waiting outside the pool gate as the pool was leased out from the school for public use and we had to have our students out in time for the maintenance people to sweep the pool. Billys problem wasn't so much he wouldn't get out to go home. He wouldn't get out even to use the bathroom as we found out the second day of summer school. He pooped in the pool. There was the biggest...well... lets call it floater. More so it was a cotillion There was a whole armada of Willys poop in the pool. Maintenance came and unhappily scooped it out and turned on the pool pump and cleaner, adding extra chlorine. This meant that all the kids standing outside waiting to use the pool would have to wait. There was a twenty four hour rule when a kid does what Willy did, it's a 24 hour wait till it can be used again. As we finally left the pool area we received a round of boos from the kids waiting. They were told the bad news. It was the first day of open pool but it would have to wait till tomorrow. Willy was banned from the pool. At the end of Wills tenure with me at this school, his Dad came to pick him up on the last day. The first time he picked him up in such a long time. He was driving the same truck smoking and making the same horrendous noise. He pulled up after the buses had pulled out Willy jumped in,

they both waved a goodbye and I haven't
seen them since.

Chapter 36
Vance

This was one big kid. Vance was a very large individual for only being twelve years old. He was six feet tall and weighed in excess of 200 lbs, more like 300. He was big. In the two years that I had Vance in my class he was responsible for a lot of excitement. His first day of school was no exception. Vance, out of the clear blue sky got up out of his desk and started hitting another student. Although he was big he didn't seem to hit hard. When he finished hitting he went straight over to an empty desk and promptly pushed it over. It was more like throwing it down. The student he hit was okay, she was crying but she was okay. Vance went back to his desk and resumed doing the task we gave him when he came in. It was over in a few seconds. We were introduced to Vinces unpredictable wild behaviors. These types of behaviors were starting to be a daily routine. It got to the point after a few months that he would have to be restrained on the floor. Being as big as he was, it took three or for adults to hold him down on the floor till he got a grip on himself and till he could control himself. I made several attempts to get him dismissed from our school. He needed to be somewhere where there could be more control of him before he actually hurt someone. I would go home physically beat. Everyday we were having a conflict and battles with Vance and he started taking our entire attention.

The cafeteria was especially difficult. He would throw food, kick some of the students from the regular classes. He loved to get a mouth full of food and spit it out on the lunch table. Even after all of his displays of weird behavior I still felt bad for him. He probably really didn't know what he was doing.

The day came when Vance arrived at school in a particularl ripe and ready mood for trouble. By lunch we had already restrained him twice. His mother refused to come to school to get him. She said it was our problem and that's what we get paid for. She was actually mostly right about that. I had made many more reports about him and request that he be moved, but after a year I made no progress. That day after his early troubles we took him to lunch.

He had settled down some and I wasn't really worried about how he would be. The caféteria was already filled with students except for our table that was saved. We were running a little behind schedule. Like most schools the cafeteria served as an auditorium as well as an eating place. There was a large stage used for programs and the music departments shows. The Curtains were pulled wide open. When we walked into the cafeteria Vance was right next to me. Vance and I crossed the threshold into the eatery, he bolted from my side and started a weird and bizarre noise. It was like a giggle, laugh and cry. He ran from me and through the cafeteria with 500 Jr. High students watching. It wasn't a matter of catching him, it was a matter for what to do with him when we did. He kicked a couple of students, he would jump up and down, laugh, giggle and cry. All the time running through the cafeteria. Vance had a hold of his waist band on his pants still running through the Auditorium. The students in the room to my surprise paid him no attention. It was still very noisy as most cafeterias are during lunch, and Vance running around with me right behind him. He got a thrill from the chase so I didn't really run after him, just tail him. Vance made his move. He jumped up on to the stage where all could see him, laughing all the time. He stopped in the exact middle of the stage still holding the top of his pants. He was wearing sweat pants so there was no belt just elastic holding the whole works up. He was stopped and for a split second just starred at the 500 or so students, but just as quickly he pulled his pants down and gave the entire audience a total and complete frontal view. With his pants down he couldn't move very fast so I jumped up and yanked his pants up and quickly pushed him off stage down the side stage entrance. Vance was much too quick for me this day. He bolted again and went through the double doors that led from the cafeteria to the office and work room. For whatever reason Vance had he went straight to the Xerox machine, made a fist and hit the top of it as hard as he could. The lid of the machine bounced up and slammed back down. Nobody on campus was getting involved . Vince did what he wanted to do. I just tailed him till help came. Being lunch time everyone was doing their own thing and my assistants were taking care of other problems with my class. After Vance Hit the Xerox machine he stopped. It was like a switch went off. He turned around walked back into the cafeteria , sat down and started eating like nothing even happened. At least the principal got to see Vance at his worst. He was hiding in his office when the freight train came through, but came out for a breif moment. He had seen enough. We made it back to class with no more problems till we got into the class and he started all over again pushing desks and throwing crayons and paint. We had to restrain him until the buses came. He was settled down enough to send home. We all took a deep breath and was left with what will happen tomorrow?

Tomorrow came and after what happened the day before we decided to have Vance eat in the class room with one of the assistants. Vance didn't have a problem with that and eating by himself seemed to settle him down, but he still had his regular disturbances, throwing things and hitting. Some of the parents were getting upset, and rightfully so. The problem was that at that time there was just no other place to put him. Toby, Willy and a couple others had the same problem of hurting and lashing out at the other students also. The problem was much bigger than Vince but he was the major challenge.

Vance came in class very quiet today and even seemed like he was a little lethargic and for a couple hours he seemed half asleep. I still wasn't able to get his mother to come to school. The principal had several phone conversations with her but she was a little hard to deal with. While Vance was at school it was her time off. Vance finally woke up and started throwing things and I called the P.E. teacher to come and help me restrain him again. Campus Security and everyone who counted came and helped. Finally the office put pressure on Vances mother to come to school and help deal with him. He was going to be suspended even though it took a year and a half to do it if the mother didn't show up. That was enough threat. Vance's mom didn't want to loose her baby sitter so we expected her the next day. Vince wasn't on the bus so we expected that he wouldn't be at school at all or his mother would bring him. Just a few minutes after all of the buses cleared out I saw Vance walking across the school grounds with who was probably his mother right behind him. It wasn't until the two of them got closer did I notice that his mother had a large thick leather strap in her hand. Vance had his undivided attention pointed at the belt. His mother came into the class with him. She said hi to me, said she was Vance's mom and if he gave me any trouble just take the strap to him. She also told me to call her if I had any more problems, and she left. I stood there with my mouth wide open. I could not believe what I just heard and saw. Of course I could not use a leather strap on Vince and wouldn't even if I was allowed. I brought the belt to the principal and explained what had occurred.

He told me there wasn't anything he could do unless I saw a mark on him or I saw her use the belt. I left the leather strap with him and left it at that. Vance was a very good student for the next two weeks. We didn't have one problem with him. Not one desk tipped over or not one student hit or kicked.

Vance was setting us up. We had a sofa in our room as sometimes one of the kids would take a nap or sometimes they weren't feeling well and needed to lay down. At times the sofa was used as a reward. If you were really good that week or did something you got to sit on the sofa for a period of class time. I just got a delivery of a cabinet to keep art supplies. It was all metal, it came in a box and I had to put it together. I had some of the higher level students help me put it together. They handed me the parts and tools when I asked them. I made a small lesson out of it, but at the same time I had to get up every now and then to take care of the other students. We had all the parts spread out all over the floor. We were about ready to put the opening mechanism on the door and noticed there was a missing part. It was a bar two feet long or so the latched the door to the frame. I went back to the box sitting by our old wood cabinet and it wasn't there. Vance was sitting at the sofa, being as quiet and good as a student could be. Sorrel another student was standing next to me by the cabinet box still looking for the missing piece. I turned and looked at Vance, and at that time he bent down, reached under the sofa and in one swift movement and in an instant, he had the missing piece in his grasp throwing it as hard as he could in our direction. It seemed like slow motion. This metal bar was coming at us at hyper speed. Before me or Sorrel could move the bar twirling and spinning went right between us and stuck in the cardboard. If that thing would have hit us it would have impelled us. It certainly could have killed Sorrel, She being a very small and more fragile young girl. Vance just looked at us and smiled. We did not over react, rather I called the principal so he could see the product of Vances violence and premeditation. After he had seen the damage and evidence of potential danger, he called the parent and a few others. When he returned to my room he told me we would not be seeing Vance anymore! And we didn't. I did find out that he was placed in what is called a non-community school. After awhile, two years or so I saw him later. He was well over six feet tall and over three hundred pounds and the new school had their hands full. He was a violent destructive student. In his case I was not sorry that he left. I was more disturbed that he was left in my class to terrorize us for so long. The rest of the students behaviors changed when he left, they were truly afraid of Vance ...and so was I.

I let Mickey go to another class. I actually had a choice. It would in some ways be a life changing decision. Mickey made everything so much easier. He made things laughable and never too serious. Why I let him go? I don't know. Big mistake, as the following chapters will reveal.

Chapter 37
Watch Your Back

This chapter is by far the hardest to write. It is not about a student nor an assistant that truly stands out as a shinning example. Rather this chapter is about those few, those very few that do their best to destroy what is good. It is about two individuals that I will not even make up a name for. I will refer to them as him and her, he and she. For the most part up to this time I have had nothing but good things happen. Some things were bizarre and some dangerous and tenous, but always the end result was positive and good, and the bad things not the result of bad people. In this case things were never good.

After the year with Vance I went through major changes in staffing as far as my classroom assistants were concerned. Summer school was ready to come about and I was to get two new assistants. I was some what excitited, but at the same time

I had lost Mikey to another class and my other assistant had moved away. The female assistant had worked off and on with me as a inexperienced substitute. I found out she had applied for the vacant position. I recommended her for the job as I would later regret. She interviewed and soon was put in my class as a full time employee. "He" was an assistant leaving another classroom for reasons that are still questionable. I had no choice but to take him. I didn't want him, as his bad reputation had preceded him. My excitement was starting to wear off.

At the same time we were to move the classroom to another building that would be closer to the restrooms. It just so happens that it was the same physical classroom that "he" had worked in previously. The class that was in there moved somewhere else. Every year was like that. You never knew where you were going to be. Never the less the summer started and both my new assistants were there. Now I hesitate calling them assistants as they didn't assist at much.

The new class room was nothing less than horrible. It was an utter complete mess. I had not been in the class to see what it needed. The teacher that was in there before had allowed my new assistant to keep a snake, which wasn't so bad but he also kept rats which he bred and fed to the snake. He never cleaned up. The room smelled like rat crap and the snake would occasionally escape. "He" had disgusting inappropriate posters covering the room walls of Ozzy Osbourne, Bloody pictures of bands, etc etc. The young lady quickly grabbed the best desk in the room and claimed it as hers. What I didn't know that these two were good friends already and with in days I could tell they had their own agenda. They were going to run that class the way they wanted to.

Even though I tried everything diplomatically possible, like taking the inappropriate pictures down one at a time, things progressively got worse exponentially. They had started calling parents on there own and doing things that only the teacher had authority to do. They were arranging field trips without my approval, the list goes on. When I gave them things to do they pretty much ignored it. It was starting to be a living hell, an unteachable class. Hind site always tells you that maybe a different approach would have been better. Me I am a easy going person and like things to work themselves out. Hindsite shows me these two were incompetent to work or be around handicapped individuals. They were incapable of following authoritative directions. I let things get too far, that is the only mistake that I made.I didn't know it but they had already strated making complaints about me and how I ran the class, Ive only been doing for 20 years by that time so what would I know. I started the year off with a good raport with all of my parents we all got along and I talked to them often. But every time they would take liberties and call a parent they would say things to them. I was never sure what but by the end it was evident that it wasn't good stuff.

They had taken every liberty they could possibly take. They would go to lunch whenever they felt like it. It was becoming a wasted year for me and the students as these two saboteurs had made it unrepairable. My plan was to make sure they would not be rehired or at the very least not work with handicapped students in this district in the future.Things would never go that far. Me and her had butted heads over a student that she was inviting in from another class. This student was violent and dangerous and I finally told her that she could not and would not bring that student back, this was after several incidences that nearly hurt my students. That must have been it for her, because from that time on it was a very cold classroom. He was still off doing his own thing and not following any kind of direction or schedule given him. When there are two people willing to conspire and lie against you there is almost nothing you can do and that is what happened to me. The most unthinkable and terrible thing that could happen to a teacher in my position. Things were falling apart and there was nothing I could tell the principal or anyone for that matter. They had gone to the principal and told her things that were so unbelievable and so incredible that it simply floored me. They had told the pricipal a month before that I had left a student in the classroom by himself. This was a student that was wheelchair bound. I only found out about this a month later after the alledged incident. The principal called me in and asked me about it. I told her I remember the day that they were talking about. But the students were to be in P.E. I was not in the class. It was for all purposes not my class at the time. The male assistant had brought the student in the class took him out of the wheelchair a put him in a place he could not be seen from the door. I was not in the class. The class is leaving for P.E. I walked in grabbed a coffe cup and walked out The male assistant was already gone. He left him there. To cover his mistake he ran down to the office with his little friend the Female assistant and proceeded to make up their story. For the next several chapters which accounts for about two years, I was in Federal depositions, answered incredible accusations of which there was not one bit of truth. Remember to watch your back. That is what I tell myself each and everyday. Because even though I have dedicated my life to special kids, spent thousands of hours,dollars and memories, there is always someone there to stab you in the back. That week that I was told of the Federal law suit , my best friend died, I was served for a personal lawsuit for a dog bite, and my wife filed for divorce and served me in my classroom, not a good week.

Chapter 38
Lesa

My class at Hook Jr. was still going through major changes. I was loosing students to the high school as they were getting older and I had news that I was getting a ton of students at the beginning of the new year so we had to make room. Toby left to Germany with his Dad, a few more had gone to the high school. There was even a couple who did not show back up or register for the new year. The two "assistants" that caused so many problems were possibly on their way out. Predictions though were that I was getting up to ten more new students. Vance was gone so that eliminated the biggest part of the problem, …..I thought. It was tough enough to start the new year with two or three new students, but one by one my new year was being filled with new and "interesting" students. Lesa was the first to show. Her mother brought her. She didn't trust the buses she said, so she would be bringing her. Lesa was adopted, and her life before she was adopted to her mother and father was one that was more tragic than I care to write about. She was a victim of the people who were supposed to love her and take care of her. Lesa was very unpredictable. She was totally up or totally down. She was rarely in between. She was either hitting, kicking, biting, cursing, etc, etc, or she was trying to put a hug on you, telling you how much she cared about you. She was extremely intelligent, not like Paulson the arsonist or the others that attended the Juvenal Hall schools. Lesa had her own brand of intelligence. She knew how to manipulate a situation and she could bend your will. She had that way about her.

Lesa could read, she could do hi level Math, but she could not control her emotions and she knew it. She used her weaknesses to her advantage.

Lesa was a big girl. She was tall and heavy for her age. She was 13 years old but she looked 16. It was always a surprise how Lesa would come dressed to school. One day she would wear a flowered Moo Moo with a lea of flowers around her neck and the next she would wear nothing less than a wedding dress and a straw hat. Nearly everyday she would put tons of make-up on. She looked like an actress from a silent film movie where they powder their faces with white flower, and blotches of red rouge on each cheek. Aside from her ability to get along with the adults most of the time she never got along with any of the other students in our class. It was a constant battle with her to stay out of fights with the others. I didn't blame her much because that is why she was in our class in the first place. We did work with her daily on keeping things under control. Her adoptive mother gave us lots of good ways to work with her like counting to ten, closing your eyes and think of happy things. For the most part these were effective tools for Lesa as long as someone was with her all the times, which of course was impossible. During her stay with us we called her parents hundreds of times. We finally realized that the best people to work with her and control her were some of the regular students that had befriended her during the course of her tenure. They turned out to be invaluable. Lesa eventually was signed up for clarinet classes at our school where eventually she was doing good. But the day came when her friends were not able to come over to the class for some reason like they were testing or the regular school kids had a different function that day. That day was bad, very bad. Sometimes when bad things happen, they happen in an instant, without warning and without provocation. Lesa was sitting quietly, at least as quiet as she could be. She stood up went to the pencil sharpener, sharpened her pencil walked over to a student we knew she did not get along with and stabbed him in the arm as hard as she could. Before we could even react she had already gotten half way to her own desk where she would eventually just sit and continue her work like nothing happened. I had immediately called the principal, the nurse, and all parents involved. Lesa mother came and Lesa maintained that she didn't do anything, but she was suspended from school indefinitely.

I had a very good relationship with Lesas' mother and family. I visited their house several times and even went to a pool party. For the longest time I still kept in contact with them but sometimes time fades friendships away. Lesa started home schooling with a tutor and the last I had heard she was doing fine. The last time I was at her house we were talking amongst us and Lesa came up to me and handed me something. Lesa gave me a key chain. She has had that key chain for most of her life. It was Part of a Karate belt that was sown together for Lesa as a memento and it meant a lot to her. Her mother was blown away. Lesa never let that thing out of her sight. She told me she wanted me to have it. I told her I couldn't because it did mean so much but she insisted. Her mother said I better take it. I took the key (belt and put my keys on it and told her that at any time she wanted it back she could have it) and that I was just borrowing it. I think that Lesa was very perceptive and sensed that this was the last time we would see each other. She was right. But I still have the key chain and this is four years later. I think of her a lot, and as for the boy who got stabbed , he was okay. Never figured out why she stabbed him and Lesa never admitted to even knowingly doing it. The Boy who got stabbed, he stabbed a girl with a pencil in the arm a year after Lesa had already been gone for sometime. We all bare our scars from that classroom.

Chapter 39
Charles

The two assistants that caused me so many problems and would eventually go to different demises were gone from my class. The young female assistant was fired or ran out and quit when she found out her little conspiracy to get rid of me didn't work. I am not sure officially what happened to her but she was gone, which was almost the best thing that could happen to handicapped children in my room. The male assistant who I had referred to as her little puppy dog was reassigned away from special children for the most part. But this was certainly not the end of my problems with the court system. It was not the end of my problems with the two conspirators, "trouble makers". For me, I was still in the classroom with my special kids. It was where I loved to be. For the next year and a half I would be performing my duties under the shadow of accusations, lies and rumors. Teachers can be cruel and can be some of the worst gossipers. All the time I did my duties, teaching and having fun with my students. I always did my job with integrity and professionally. My objective never changed, even with the new students I would be getting in my class knowing that things could change for me at moments notice.

If someone would have told me that I was back working at the mental institution that I had volunteered at 20 years ago I would have believed them. The students I was getting were different, not like the "normal" mentally handicapped. Charles my newest student was coming to me soon. I had a chance to read his file and it was a foot thick, literally. I was told by the psychologist that I needed to go to the district office for the meeting. There is not much one can prepare for when you attend a student meeting. I have just learned that you need to anticipate anything. I got to the meeting room early, before the parents and the student showed up. As I sat there with the others, the psychologist, Assistant Superintendent, Nurse, Behavioralist, ten others in all I went over the files one more time. It read like the tales of a psychotic teenager. It was not really believable. The mother of Charles walked in with her son. From the very start she took total control of the meeting. She had obviously been around the block with different school districts She went on and on and on till she could not talk any more. She talked or should I say rambled for one solid hour and did not say one coherent sentence. We started asking our normal and regular questions like what schools and programs he had gone to. Each time we asked a question she would go on for another 15 to 20 minutes, it was endless. Charles who appeared to be very aware and capable was not allowed to talk. The one time we asked him a question he started to answer and his mother finished his sentence and paragraph. The time came when the nurse had a chance to ask her routine questions about his health, had he had his shots?, had he ever been sick?, allergies? Then she asked does he take any medication? That was the question that opened Pandora's box. When she came into the meeting room she had a large paper grocery bag which she put down by her feet. When the Nurse asked her question she quickly pulled the bag up on the table and dumped it out. Out came every kind of drug you could imagine, Thorizine, Ritilin, and at least twenty other different kinds. They were all in pharmacy type containers, and they all looked like they were prescribed, at least at one time or another. She proceeded to tell us that these are the medications that he takes but she forgets how much and when he supposed to take them. This was our first clue what was wrong with Charles. Four hours into the meeting Charles's mother tells us that she is not sure that she trust our school and that she would like to come to visit. Of course, we said, knowing that we couldn't deny her anyway. A visitation day was set up and they both would be coming in a few days. She gathered up her drugs and left as quickly as she came in. After she was gone and nearly five hours later we all looked at each other and didn't say a word. I went back to my classroom where I had only an hour left and prepared my two new assistants of what was coming.

I prepared my assistants for the coming of Charles's mother and for Charles. I wasn't sure yet if we were even going to get him as a student. Sure enough they both showed up on the third day after our revealing meeting. They stopped at the office to check in. The principal was not at the meeting so she had no idea what was walking in. I tried to warn her but you had to be there to get full understanding of what was to come. After checking in they both worked there way to my classroom, they came in and started talking about how she wanted things this way and that, and how her son does not associate with this kid or that kid and he is to be with me the entire time he is at school, and if she decides to send him here. It wouldn't have broken my heart if she decided not to send him to our school except that Charles really was a neat kid, when his mother wasn't there. Our (her) conversation went on for a few hours, until she got every detail out that she wanted to say. They left as quickly as they showed up and told me as she left that she would let me know if she would send him here or not. I had stranded the rest of the students for the entire time she was there. She demanded every split second.

Two weeks went by and we hadn't heard a word about Charles and surmounted that we were not picked as the lucky class. But not long after I received a call from the principal that Charles would be there "tomorrow". The next day came and it was already an hour over and the office called and told me Charles and his mother were there to start school. They would be at my room in a couple of minutes. The office told me to be prepared for what was coming. I wasn't sure what they meant by that but when I saw Charles and his mother approach the classroom then I understood. When a parent signs in to visit or come to the classroom they get a stick on name tag. There was no place to put here tag as what she was wearing, there wasn't much of. She had taken the name tag and stuck it directly over her cleavage and directly on her skin. I thought that was very unusual. If it was for shock value, she got it but we didn't let her know it. She stayed the entire rest of the day. She talked, talked, talked, talked. I didn't have one moment with one other student. Charles was still not allowed to talk. Not even when I could get him in a lesson group. His mother followed him around, sat with him at the lesson tables and even answered some of the lesson questions for him. This wasn't working but I understood what I was working with and put faith in that things would relax a bit.

Slowly we saw less of Charles's mother and more of him. When mother wasn't there Charles would open up and it got hard to keep him quiet when he was supposed to be. We had on going problems though with Charles's mother as Charles would go home and tell her all sorts of things. He would make up wild stories about other students hitting him or stealing things from him. When he did that, mother would be there the next day questioning me for hours. That was getting very old but it was part of working in a class like ours. Sometimes the parents are more disabled then their kid we have in class.

Charles's mother always wore the same dress to school visits. I think it was probably her only dress. After she had worn her name tag over her breasts the one time the principal had told her to please not do that again so her visits after that she would stick it to the side of her face. So she would come to school off and on and her name tag on her cheek.

I worried about all the students at one level or another and I was concerned about Charles the most. After our initial meeting I was never sure if he was getting the proper medication or if he was supposed to get any at all. He had a lot of mood swings. One day he could barely stay awake and the next he was bouncing off of the walls. He had one particularly bad day. He came to class with a real bad attitude, calling other students bad names and being physical. I tried to talk to him and he started pushing me. He wouldn't let me get near him. Finally he pushed another student so hard it knocked her over. I had to restrain him as he was getting crazy. I had my assistant call security. It would be awhile before they got there, so I had to hold him. He was a very strong boy. While I was holding him down and away from the other students I smelled the unmistakable odor of alcohol. Charles was drunk or at least had a pretty good buzz. His mother was called and she got there an hour later. Her problem wasn't that Charles was obviously drinking but that

I had to restrain him. She was very angry. She took Charles home and a few days later the child protection agency showed up at their house. She was very street smart and wouldn't allow them in. She knew every right she had and how to use them to her advantage. She also knew her time was up at that school. I had Charles about 5 months. I don't think we had one day of that time that was not disturbed by his mother in one way or another. Charles showed up a couple of days here and there and one day never saw him again. I did get a call from a school principal in New Mexico asking some very detailed questions about Charles and his mother. She was evidently there causing the same problems she caused us. Charles was never a problem. Away from his mother he was one my best students ever. I wish things could have been different for him.

I was becoming more concerned about the allegations my two former assistants made. Now, formally the parents of the student that the male assistant left in the class were making a written complaint and took it to a lawyer.

Chapter 40
Erin

A boy that got lost in the shuffle with all of the daily excitement was Erin. He could the be source of classroom turmoil at times but his was usually overshadowed by one of the others. Erin had very smooth and almond colored skin, He was a very good looking boy. He was unfortunately autistic like Leti. But like Leti he had certain abilities. He would never forget anything you told him, nor would he forget anything you showed him. He had unlike Leti very bad printing and when he made a mistake he would not correct it, he would write the same mistake forever. Erin could count and add and subtract. Sometimes he would add large numbers up in his head and he would surprise us with the right answer. On some days though things weren't clicking right in his head and he would come to school having a bad day. He would hold his head tightly and scream that he was having a head ache. He would yell out for "Mary" who we believed was his foster mother. Erin would yell out at the top of his voice to call the police. These episodes could go on for hours or minutes. He would just snap out of them. When this would happen and we had a larger problem like Vance throwing metal objects at us, Erins' problems were swept under the carpet until other more immediate matters could be dealt with. I had Erin in my class for nearly the entire time I was at the Jr. high school and always amazed me to see some of the things he could do. Erin had an insatiable desire to throw small rubber balls and bounce them. When he did, I rarely saw him miss catching it. If he missed he would look at the ball as though there was something wrong with it. When we wanted Erin to settle down from an episode we gave him a ball and let him go right outside and cool off. He could be right outside our class for hours. As long as we could see him we were okay with it. The bouncing ball thing was not the thing that he liked to do the most. When not bouncing a ball, he was juggling dimes. He always had a couple of coins in his pocket to juggle but he preferred dimes. He would spend hours at home taking two dimes throwing them up high and hitting them with the palm of his hand in a way that they always came down together in the palm of his hand in the same place. His bizarre ability to do this wasn't the strangest part though. He would throw the dimes up and together in one motion kick the two dimes with his foot and catch them in his hand. He would do this every so often. But he never missed.

Erin did not like being touched, as a lot of autistic students do not like being touched, or someone being too close. After the years I had been working with him I had gained enough trust that I was allowed in his space and was allowed to share his world. Occasionally he would have a conversation with me when he could come into my world and not me in his. I saw Erin about a year later in a store. He saw me and waved, and said hi and called me by my name. He remembered me and I knew he always would as he never forgot anything. I think if I saw him today he would still know me by name, and I his, for friends like him you never forget.

Chapter 41
Matt

You could call Matt, "Mister dependable." I could trust him to take notes to the office, go to lunch by himself, and do almost anything that I asked him to. He was a student who had much of the same likes that I had. We both liked to garden and we both liked to go fishing. We would sit in the classroom and talk about our trips to the lake and how to bait a hook. He told me every day how his garden was doing. He lived in an apartment so his garden wasn't very big, but the guy knew what he was doing. He brought us tomatoes and Zuccini on a regular basis. That year we asked the principal if Matt and I could use a little piece of property on the school ground that was away from all of the other classes for a garden. This would be his garden that we would grow together. I showed him how to plan it an draw up a plan. We wrote a list of things we needed and got started.

Matt had no idea how much work even a small garden can be but he was a hard worker and was determined to have the best garden around. We dug and roto tilled, fertilized and watered and we were ready to plant. Hank and I planted Corn, Zuccini, Tomatoes, Watermelon and String Beans. It dosnt sound very exciting but for Matt, he was in seventh heaven. I too felt a certain bonding with him working together and later seeing the fruit of our labor. The garden sprung up quickly. The regular students knew not to touch anything in our plot. It was like a sanctuary. I almost spent too much time with Matt, almost neglecting the other students, so we got the okay to start another late garden that the whole class would be involved in. It wasn't as good as Matts garden but they all got experience getting a little dirty. Matt got in the routine of getting to school and going right to the watering and weeding. He would spend half of the day by himself working and tending to the gardens needs. He even made a little money selling corn and tomatoes to the teachers on campus. Fishing was something I never got to do with him. I never seemed to get the time to hook up with him. Matt moved on to high school. And I finished off one more year at the Jr. High School. I would see his father at the Wal-Mart from time to time as he worked there and I went to that store quite often. Matt was content at the high school. He made new friends and new teachers would have the same opportunity to meet a genuine, really good kid.

A couple of years later I was assigned to the high school where Matt was attending and we struck up a friendship again. I see him nearly every day now in the morning and we talk about going fishing together. One of these days we will actually go. Matt was out for a few weeks and when he came back he told me his mother passed away and that he was living with his sister. His Mom and Dad got a divorce between the time that he came to the high school and when I got assigned here. Matt is a resilient and happy young man. This year, Matt will graduate from high school and will be going to the Jr. College in town. He told me he is going to take gardening and sell vegetables at the college produce market. I will be checking in on him from time to time to make sure he is doing okay. When I was done writing this chapter I read it to him and he just replied "that's me!"

Chapter 42
Hank

There were two things that I learned about working with mentally handicapped students, and they were that every student is uniqully different, and whatever could happen will happen, or did I mention that before? With Hank, that was no exception. Hank came to our class one day, he just showed up as a new student without much warning. He had no speech and made noises with his mouth. He was thin but very solid and stood at 5'5" or so. Hank loved to throw spit. When sitting at his activity table he would dig two fingers in his mouth, get a wad of spit and fling it as far as he could. This was unfortunate for the student sitting across from him. We found early on that his seat would have to be placed away from others and he would flip saliva onto the washable wall on a regular basis.The wall became a daily chore, everything we tried to get him to stop failed and accepted the fact that he was going to do it regardless. There was one incident though that made me think of Hank, besides his mother that worked at the local candy shop, the giver of frequent out of date candy which we did eat and share with the students. There was this incident in the cafeteria. Hank was generally cooperative at the food center. He was very sloppy but he would always sit quietly and attend to his eating, till one day! This was burrito day, a bean burrito. Hank had only been with us for a couple of weeks and we hadn't had burrito day yet. Hank sat with his food. The cafeteria was full of students from the regular class rooms, a couple of hundred students at least. Hank decided this would be a good time to stand up, pick up his burrito, split it in half and threw its contents all over everyone in front of him and beyond. Within seconds he finished his lunch off by throwing it, milk, salad, string beans, everything in every direction. Unlike when Vance flipped out in the cafeteria and the regular students were well behaved and ignored the distraction, every student broke out into a spontaneous food fight. It was awful. We helped the custodians clean up after lunch. It was an absolute disaster.

Hank continued his remaining time at our school eating lunch by himself and a helper in the class room where he never threw a bean burrito again.

Even after Hank graduated from our class we would always see his mother at the candy store and she would sneak us a little bit of sweets and she would thank us for taking care of her boy. She knew how hard it could be, and like most parents were usually very appreciative. I would always thank them for having the opportunity.

Finale

As I wrote and remembered so much of the events and people over the past twenty years or so, memories started sprouting. There is another group of kids somewhere in my head. I am going to write about them too. All these kids and people are real. These things really happened. They occupied most of my life and certainly made my life better. Tommy Allen where are you? He is out there somewhere still banging his head no doubt. To be sure there is a teacher with him helping him and guiding him. I still hear the swing creeking and whinning back and forth, back and forth.

Thank you to my wife Linn for all of her loving and devoted support.